Haven't Any News

Ruby's Letters from the Fifties

Haven't Any News

Ruby's Letters from the Fifties

To Una — a good soat Cook from a writer about good food — best wishes

Edna Staebler

Letters written by **Ruby Cress**

Edited by her sister, **Edna Staebler**

With an Afterword by **Marlene Kadar**

Wilfrid Laurier University Press

WLU

Canadian Cataloguing in Publication Data

Cress, Ruby, 1911-
    Haven't any news : Ruby's letters from the
fifties

ISBN 0-88920-248-6

1. Cress, Ruby, 1911-   – Correspondence.
2. Housewives – Ontario – Correspondence.
I. Staebler, Edna, 1906-   .   II. Kadar, Marlene,
1950-   .   III. Title.

HQ759.C74 1995   305.4′092   C95-931028-2

Cover design: Jose Martucci, Design Communications

Front cover photograph: Ruby in 1954
Back cover photograph: Ruby with her family

♾

Printed in Canada on recycled paper

Contents

Introduction to Ruby's Letters

by her sister, Edna Staebler

In our childhood family of Mother, Daddy, and my two younger sisters, Jan and Ruby, we always told Mother everything: where we went, what we did, and what we thought. Perhaps that is why—when we were grown up and separated—frequently writing letters was like talking to each other.

When Ruby married Fred in 1940 they lived in Halifax. Their children, Sally and Billy, were born there, far from London, Ontario, where the rest of us lived all our lives.

Ruby wrote letters home almost every week. In 1947 when she and her little family moved to the edge of Barrie, Ontario, and we occasionally visited one another, her letters came just as often. She wrote about anything that came into her head: her children, her husband, her friends, social activities, her housekeeping, food, clothes, schemes for making money—which was scarce in her household—her dreams for the future. She wrote: "So help me, why don't I have talent? Why can't I write stories or paint pictures? I'd like to do something to become famous so I could make money and travel." Her letters were always enthusiastic, lively, funny, or poignant. We'd read them to each other on the phone or pass them around. Often we saved them.

Then one day—probably in the fall of 1957—I thought: "Ruby IS a writer, she's writing all the time: if her letters were edited and published other people could enjoy them as much as we do and Ruby might earn enough money to make her dreams come true. Wouldn't that be fabulous?"

The idea excited me. I asked Mother and Jan to save all Ruby's letters and give them to me as they came. Throughout the 1950s they filled a carton.

I started to work. I changed all the names of people and the locale of the cities where we live. I didn't change Ruby's erratic spelling or syntax. I didn't rewrite, but I did rearrange, leaving out boring bits about household chores or some things Ruby saw through the window when she sat writing at her kitchen table. Many letters that were much like each other I left out altogether. I spent over a year working on Ruby's letters. That was 40 years ago and I can't remember everything I did or why. I just tried to make them a good read.

Now I'm sorry to tell that in March 1959, when I was busy with my own life and journalistic assignments, I put Ruby's edited letters into my filing cabinet, and when I moved to my cottage on Sunfish Lake, I burned the carton of originals!

One evening last winter after reading a prize-winning Canadian novel about the life of a family, I was disappointed and feeling blah. When I went to bed I took the packet of Ruby's letters out of my cabinet drawer and started to read them. I kept reading until two in the morning. The story of Ruby's loving, eager young family made me feel good. The letters — intimate, cheerful, and gutsy — made me laugh, and almost made me cry. The years since the 1950s had given them another dimension: they were now social history, informative, revealing, and fun to read.

I asked several English professors, a publisher, and three generations of friends and relations to read Ruby's letters: all of them told me they couldn't put them down and wished there had been more.

Ruby didn't know I had edited her letters. Before the process of publication could begin her permission had to be given. After she read them she wondered if they might embarrass her two grown-up children, if readers would think she was stupid because of her poor spelling, if the people next door whose little boy had picked her tulips and tomatoes might sue her for defamation of character.

Ruby was assured that all the names in the book could remain anonymous and her family surname could be used on the copyright page instead of her married one. With some hesitation she agreed to the publication and now considers the book the beginning of a great adventure. She told me, "I'll be 84 years old and I'm not going to worry about what people say about the book. I'm just going to dream about what I'll wear if it wins the Governor General's Award."

Ruby's Letters

by Ruby Cress

Dear Kay

     Sometimes I get so darn mad at Fred. Here he is with a Master's degree in Math from Western and he's smart and can do far more things at the office then some of the others down there in the figuring line but he just can't sell insurance and he won't stop and do something else. That's the worst of it. I'd like him to try teaching school — he has so much patience and he loves kids but do you think he'll do it? NO . . . He did take a test one time when I made him and the man said he wouldn't have strick enough disopline for a school teacher — but why couldn't he? He's got the brains. He talked about going into farming with Mac and Myrtle but he never was interested in farming when he was a boy, could hardly wait to get out of it — so why go back now and maybe we'd have to live in a house without plumming and I'd have to learn to milk cows. Better stay here and scrimp. Fred says money isn't everything anyway.

     Thanks again for the basket of fruit you sent us from Florida, I still have two oranges which the kids will be eating at noon. Aren't we lucky to have such a grand family as ours? Look at Fred's family — his sister Belle never writes, Myrtle writes me once in a while but she's just like company when I do see her — and Bert never comes. They never have had fun like us, so I guess they don't know the difference, but I'd die if I didn't have you birds. Oh I know I get mad at times when I go home and I swear I won't go back again — it seems when I see your nice houses and how much more money you and Janet and Mother have that I get sort of jealous and say horrid things that I'm oh so sorry for after. But each time I forget and go back because I know I'd miss all the fun if I didn't.

     Going home for Xmas, that you've never experienced — all of you living right there in London — but with us it's the best time of all. Sally and Billy get so excited, and I do, and I think even Fred does a little. Getting ready weeks ahead, clothes to pack, presents to wrap, the good-byes here, Merry Xmas to all left behind, breakfast so early and visiting friends and relations along the way — those are some of the thrills that go with it. I can hardly wait till it's Xmas again — a long time from now — with what all in between, eh?

Love, Ruby

Sept 14/50

Dear Mum

Here's what's going to happen. We're going to make the kids sleep upstairs by themselves. They both have their own beds and there's no reason why they shouldn't stay in them. We're going to see if putting our foot down won't stop this silly business of them trotting around nites. We're too easy with them and let them get away with it. Billy's five and Sally is seven-going-on-eight and should have some sence if she's ever going to. We must stop them now or we'll be sleeping with them till they're seventeen years old.

I'm sick of going to bed every nite with the kids. Fred and I have our own room downstairs but every nite we have to go up and sleep in the kid's beds. Billy's not so bad to sleep with, he doesn't move, but Sally is a kicker — she flings her arms round and hits your face and grabs you and jerks her knees in your stomach.

It's the same thing every nite. We help them undress and we tuck them in and listen to their prayers and kiss them goonight and lie with them till they're quite and we think they're asleep, then we sneak down to the living-room and we're hardly sitting before one of them yells and wakens the other one and they both come running down and say they want a drink or they have to go to the toilet.

What can we do about it? We give them water and we let them go to the bathroom, then we take them up and lie with them till they're breathing sleepy, then we creep down again. And not five minutes later we hear feet on the steps and one or the other peeks round the door and says, When are you coming to bed?

We blame it on ourselves for not being FIRM with them. We let them walk all over us. But tonight, up they go, both of them, and that's that. If they come down, up they go again until they know we mean business. It's about time.

Love
Ruby

Sept. 21/50

Dear Mother

Please don't send us money to buy another bed. Fred and I talked it over and we think it would be nuts to have four beds in one room. Those kids will just have to get used to sleeping upstairs without us and that's all that's to it. I think they're getting a little bit better since we keep bouncing them back up there when they come down at nite. We'll just have to show our athority more than we have been. They have to learn sooner or later we're the boss of them and if we don't start now, so help us, when will they learn?

And don't worry about them, mother, they're not poor little things that need to be pitied. Sure they're skinny, but that's cause they're wiry, not cause they aren't well fed. I'll see that they get enough sleep too and everything else that kids their age need. We'll train them yet and we won't spank them either. They've just got to stay put and that's all.

There's nothing wrong with that upstairs room. It may seem like an attic because it's not finished off and the side walls are low but it's warm and a good size, with windows on both ends. Kay and Janet slept there when they visited us and I don't think they got hibrofobia or anything like that, did they? In another year Sally will be begging for her own private room. What we'll do then is build shelves round the stairwell to divide the room so each kid has their own part. They seemed quite pleased with our talk at noon today about having their own rooms with doors and their own curtains and a place for their own toys, etc. See what happens.

Haven't any news. I've a cherry pie in the oven. Fred sold a policy last week and one this week — he thinks he's doing OK. I wrote — or rather Fred wrote for me — to complain about Baker's cocoa box lids; they always drop into the can. A man we know said sometimes when someone complains about a thing like that the company sends a year's supply of their product, so here's hoping they send us some cocoa. I'd make brownies, chocolate cakes, fudge. Wouldn't that be super?

Love

Ruby

Jan. 26/51

Dear Jan

Lucky day yesterday. Mac and Myrtle were here and gave us 2 chickens, 3 turnips and material to make a plad skirt for Sally from an old skirt of Myrtle's. And then your parcel arrived. Thanks so very much. I love all the stuff and Sally is thrilled with what Judy's grown out of. She came home after four and saw the coat and dresses and showed them to all the neighbour's kids. Everything fits her.

Haven't any news. I may have some soon but all is a big secret at present. Geeeeee what news if it does happen. Oh no, not a baby! Oh no, not that. I hope I've passed that stage. No this is something else. I guess I shouldn't have even mentioned it — I've been trying not to. I'll tell you as soon as I can. We've our fingers crossed. Don't tell mum, I haven't said a word to Kay either and I don't want Fred to know I even said I had a secret but I'm so excited.

Honest, Jan, Dad really is the most wonderful man, everybody says how lucky I am having such a salt of the earth. He really is, he never gets mad at me. I can truly say he's never said one cross word to me in our whole married life. And I tell people I don't have to worry about going to heaven when I die because I've got heaven on earth. I'm just so so lucky,

The sun's coming out now. The Rogers are coming for supper and bridge after. We owe them 2 meals and a perm she gave Sally and me. I shouldn't have ask them tonite I'm suppose to go to church to practice for a skit the ladies axilery is putting on. I have to make sangridges, take pickles and read the scripture, say 2 lines in the skit and dress up like a Japanese girl. These church groups sure rope you in, don't they? They asked me to convene a booth at the Baby Band tea in May too.

Here's Sally. She took her lunch to school today and ate it on her way home because none of the other kids brought theirs and she was lonesome. I knew she'd be home. Two hours is a long time playing at school during the noon hour. They are having a wonderful time these days in our front yard — they made an igloo and they go in and out, in and out.

Now she wants dinner — beef, carrots, potatoes and tossed salad. I must send my recipe for tossed salad to Women's Day. I might win $15.

Love Ruby

4 \

Feb. 8/51

Dear Jan

　　The secret is out, And I mean OUT. It was to have been an oil burner for our furnace. Fred sold a 20,000 policy to a plummer and to help make the sale Fred said he'd buy an oil burner which normally he wouldn't be for some time. But no, the plummer didn't want to put an oil burner in here, said he'd only make $25 out of it which Fred and I think he's pulling a leg.

　　He was the meanest customer. He's had Fred out on a limb for months. He'd say he'd be right up to the office and Fred would wait for him and he wouldn't come. Fred waited all Sat. morning for him to come in and he didn't show up. Fred phoned him and he said he'd phone him back sometime between then and bed time to let him know. He called at 8 oclock on Sat. nite and said he'd come Mon. morning first thing at 9. He didn't come. At 3 oclock he said he'd be in in a few minutes. He didn't get in till 5.30. Really he was the most inconsiderate person and Fred had to stay around and have it hanging over his head. It was a terrible month, this was all Fred sold and then the guy didn't buy it in January so Fred could have it added to the end of the Club year, he waited till February 2 and now Fred can't have the credit for it on his year to get a bonus. Gee some people are born mean. Poor Fred, he gets awful breaks at times. This has been a terrible strain.

　　Too bad we didn't get the oil burner, sure would have been nice for me, the cellar is always so dusty from ashes. Don't say anything about a secret to me in a letter — maybe Fred didn't want me to tell about it. He has the plummer's signed check but the guy has to go to the doctor tonite for a medical, he's 59 years old and will he pass the test?

　　Boy, is it ever getting dark outside. Darker and darker. Looks as if the world were coming to an end. It's only 10 to 4 but looks like 7.30. I need a light. I'm getting scared, it's so dark. I wish my children were home from school.

Love Ruby

/ 5

April 24/51

Dear Kay

They're singing on the radio Enjoy Yourself, it's later then you think. Guess they're playing that specially for me today — my 40th birthday. That song sure makes sence. I guess I'll just enjoy myself from now on. They say Life begins at 40 so maybe things might start happening to me. Fred sold a 5000 last nite, maybe he'll start getting breaks. A chap promised to phone him today and a man he picked up asked him to see him Friday about some insurance. Things look brighter.

I even think the sun's going to shine today, the paper said warmer. Thanks for the darling birthday card and the compact; I'd rather have had it then anything if you'd asked what I wanted and needed. It is a luxury to me cause I have only that very old wee one I had in collegiate. I love it and many many thanks. And for the card with the kitten in the hammock — wish we had a really one, don't you?

I must get at dresser drawers. I've been putting them off ever since house-cleaning talk has been going around. Was asked and refused to be a phone caller for Mission Band and for Federation group at church. I figured I'd be phoning all the time instead of getting my braided rug done this year. I'm at a dandy now: I wanted it navy and red but it's sort of rosy instead, for the bathroom. It's made out of Sally and the Smith and Rogers kids' navy and fawn wool stockings dyed. Nice to work with, soft and warm.

Thanks again for all you gave me. I like everything. I wear the slippers, use the compact, I wear your coat and I've worn your dress to four special occasions and got compliments for it. I wish you birds would visit us sometime, I met a dame who writes for radio and I'd like to have her in to talk to you, I think she'd enjoy it and you might get a kick out of it too but if I leave it go too long I may not have the nerve to invite her.

Now I'd better hop along and get my work done. We haven't eaten in the dining room since Fred made me a table and bench in the kitchen and the old washing machine's been taken to the cellar, I love it here at the table where I can sit and watch what's going on outside on the road — a pleasure but a time waster.

Love, Ruby

April 26/51

Dear Mum

It's a really rainy day and all I can think about is fishworms. How can I grow them and get the kids interested in them? I think I could make a fortune selling wigglers if I only knew how to raise them. There'd be no end of sales of them here on the highway cause hundreds of tourists go by and if they're wanting worms we'd have first chance because we're out on the edge of town. There are worm places farther along; last year we tried to get some and had a terrible time because none of them had them in stock — they didn't really grow them they just caught them and hadn't enough. I think the trade would be good — the smell too, says Fred. Dead fishworms do kick up quite a stink but we won't let them die. I'd have to learn how to raise them and feed them etc. I was digging parsnips in the garden this morning before the rain came and I saw dozens of them. I'm keen and excited about it. Some woman out in B.C. is making a selling proposition out of them so why couldn't I? She grows them for top-soil, I want them for fish. If you should hear or read anything about raising them, let me know. I should be starting now to produce for the summer trade. The kids can catch them and sell them as well as me, it would sharpen them up and give them a hobby.

A Worm Farm. Gee it would be fun. I'd have a log book to write in where all my customers came from and what all they did. I bet we'd meet some interesting people.

I'll be a worm farmer. I'm anxious to get started, but beans — tomorrow I have to help clean someone else's house. A dame in our church group has to have an operation next week so the gang of women are going to her place to do her apartment so she can go and come from the hospital knowing it's clean. She's got something wrong with her neck gland — probably not much — she's a whiner and a bossy thing. Her husband died during an operation so I guess she's scared. He was a swell chap, a good church worker but henpecked. I don't know how I let the girls rope me into this thing but anyway I said I'd pitch in — wish I could talk them into helping me finish my housecleaning.

It sure is raining hard. Do you think I will worm farm? I keep shoving Fred, he needs pushes and so do I. If I could only keep enthused about life, I'd keep him up on his toes. Maybe the worms will do it.

Love, Ruby

/ 7

April 28/51

Dear Jan

We've eaten asparagrass out of the garden and Mac and Myrtle killed a pig and sent us ribs, sausage, liver and a loin roast.

We had a meeting here Friday — 14 people — all sat round the room in a perfect circle. I couldn't have gotten more in. I must ask more people to come here. I sorta like entertaining now that I had that gang on Friday. I cleaned the house so well — waxed and polished the floors, washed the curtains. Oh I really got going — it's company that gets one at things that should be done,

Yesterday we went fishing. Fred said we were only practising cause the season isn't open yet and we didn't catch any. We had fun, took the Hade kids along. We went to Sunday school first, one kid in my class got sick and made everyone else feel that way too and another kid yelled and cried for her mother, I thought she was sick too but she just had to go to the bathroom. I got her off in a hurry — but I might have been a bit late?????? I didn't follow her to find out.

Guess what? Our neighbour's mother cat — here most of the time — had one kitten. She is grey tiger and the kitten is brown tiger like it's dad and she had it four doors away but brought it here and put it in our wood box down cellar. No one knows when or how she did it. I opened the garage doors and there was the cat and her baby. She's so sweet and gentle and so tiny herself. Four months ago she had 2 kittens and lost both. Poor little thing.

Things are sure growing. We haven't cleaned up the yard yet and we're the only ones around here with storm windows still on. Must do dishes now. Have to wash mitts, old sox, kid's woolen stuff. I should iron too. Oh there's so much to do these days it's fun deciding what to do first, one has such a choice. I love our new-painted diningroom yellow walls with the turquoise vase with the fish that Dot gave me against it and that painting that Harry did with the barn and the snow and the fence running across the front of it. Beautiful.

Must do dishes now. Oh oh the power's off — I hope it's not a two day affair — no it's on again.

Love, Ruby

May 26/51

Dear Mother

This afternoon I decided to plant some things and reached up on the veranda shelf to get the trowl and I caught my ring, ripped out my diamond and it bounced on the railing, hit an empty bag of potatoes and I never saw it again. At first I said to myself, oh this will be easy, I'll just find it — but when I went down to hunt it on the ground I couldn't see it anywhere. I got Fred's old glasses on and the magnifine glass and then I got excited and fussed and nearly cried, and I prayed, and then I went in and phoned Fred to come home from the office to help me hunt. He came right away. I was out there hunting like mad when he walked up the path and asked me what happened and I told him and as he was coming up the steps he bent down and looked in a crack and said THERE IT IS! Just like that. He didn't even look anywhere else — he found it first shot. It happened so quickly. I thanked him and thanked God.

My diamond was just stuck on dirt — old dusty maple tree keys. If it had been over a teeny bit farther it would have gone down between the house and the porch and I'd have hunted in the grass and the bridlereath bushes all the rest of my life. Fred went in to get the tweezers. I asked him if he was nervice and he said NO — one little wrong move might have nocked it down the crack for good. I was too unsteady to try it — Fred just leaned over and THERE IT WAS! A prayer answered is all I can say. I sure believe in prayer. I'll never forget when you had your heart condition how hard I prayed to make you better. I use to go to your door at nite to hear if you were breathing — I sure believe in prayer.

We're having a thunder storm right now — thundering above me — but not bad, no rain, only a heat sorta lightening. Our lilacs are out — they're lovely and more then ever. My tulips are dying.

Oh I just can't get over my diamond. A miracle.

Love

Ruby

Dear Kay

This is some poetry Sally wrote — do you think you could get it published?

Butterflies

dear little butterflies
up in the sky
oh to have wings like yours
so I could fly

Buttercup

buttercup, oh buttercup
dancing in the sun
I will come another day
when my work is done

buttercup oh buttercup
I have come again
to jump and play and dance all day
in sunshine or in rain.

Easter

easter is a happy time,
for little girls and boys
for easter rabbits hop around
and leave them lots of toys.

A snowflake

the snowflake comes softly down
in the country or the town
in the fields and in the street
to be trampled on by feet

The robin

There are some robins in the treetop
high above my head
they are singing cheer-up
time to get out of bed.

Rabbit

Once I saw a rabbit hopping
through the snow
he stopped and turned,
and looked and jumped
not knowing where to go.

Chickens

Chickens are plump, big and round
chickens are yellow black and brown.

Fairy land

Fairy land is far away,
over fields and hills
over roofs and houses
far beyond the mills.

What do you think? Would somebody pay her money for them? I think they're pretty good for a kid only 9, don't you? Are there any children's magazines?

Love Ruby

Dear Kay

Mabel gave me this notepaper, she didn't like it cause it's pink. Can't say I'd buy it myself. She got it on sale but doesn't write letters and thought I could use it up on my family. I hope you don't mind.

I'm in bed and it's only 8 oclock. I've had a cold and I'm trying to get rid of it. I stayed in bed Thurs. Fri. and Sat. mostly but it didn't help. Fred made mustard plasters for me but no go. I phoned the doctor and he gave me medicine that's so terrible it makes me dizzy and I'm scared to take it.

I worked hard today. Maybe too hard for my own good. I washed 8 sheets, pillow cases and other regular stuff, refilled the machine with clean water and started over again. I picked 8 boxes of raspberries and Fred helped me preserve 12 quarts after dinner. We've 36 quarts now and 4 baskets of cherries canned with the pits in so kids can count how many they've eaten. This sure is the time for doing stuff. You should see our berries, big as my thumb; everyone says they've never seen the like. I'll be giving you some. Fred got up at 5 this morning and picked 2 six-quart baskets full. Tomorrow jelly and ironing is my skedule. We're eating things from our garden now — a 6 quart basket of beans on Sunday — Fred ate nothing but — I ate beets and carrots as well. We don't spend money on meat.

I must ask Chester behind us to come in for supper some day. He phoned to say Mabel was in hospital. High blood pressure. Soon as she's got something to go to or do she's OK, soon as she sits at home she's all tense with nerves.

I read Ethel Water's story. Boy she sure had quite a life when young. I haven't a thing to write about, and what I wanted most to tell you I almost forgot. Thanks a million for the new slip. I love it and wear it for special. It sure is the nicest one I've ever owned. I hate to wear it under a dress it's so beautiful. You sure are good to me and I'll never be able to pay you back. Chester's in insurance too and he says business is getting harder and harder to find.

Love Ruby

Ethel Water was a performer who sang and acted on New York stages.

Dear Kay

I'm so excited about the coat you ordered for me. My first new coat since I've been married — 12 years. I've always wanted a Harris tweed and navy is just the color too cause most of my things are navy — least I've a navy hat and dress. And remember you're not paying for it. I am. I've exactly $74 in the bank so all I need extra is $1 and Fred can give me that.

Gee it's wonderful. I'm so thrilled cause I've kept thinking What will I wear this winter, I need a coat so badly. The grey one of yours you gave me is really too big, too long wasted and my coon that I've had since high school is as shabby as an old barn dog. But now, glory be, I'll be having a NEW one. When I get it and go to Western Alumnae dinner with Fred I won't feel ashamed. If only I had my B.A. too — how often I've wished I had that. I hope both my kids will one day get their's. I must tell them to concentrate hard and not let their minds run round in the cornfields like Mr. Muslin at London Collegiate said that mine did.

We've really been busy. I had the two school teachers in on Sunday for turkey and they gave us a pound of chocolates. Last nite Sally and I went to a mother and daughter banquet — she looked so cute in her middy. I washed this morning and baked 3 pies — wish you lived near us and I'd bring you one. This aft I made over slacks of mine for Sally and recovered her eiderdown, this morning I cleaned, washed up the bathroom and kitchen and waxed floors. Now I'm tired and fat. Wish I were slim and figurey for my new coat.

I only hope it fits. But with measurements taken all round surely the salesgirl can tell the size I need — waist 28, chest 34, hip 37 (isn't that horrible?) sleeves 27, skirt length 43. I know a 16 is too big, even at my fattest I've never been a 16. A 14 should be just right, shouldn't it? I should be a 12.

Oh — I nearly forgot — the most important thing — Fred gets the cast off his broken ankel today. Beans, darn it, I wanted to take a picture of it but there's no sun and I've no film for the camera.

Love, Ruby

Middy: A loose blouse with a square sailor collar worn by children, women and sailors.

Dear Kay

My new coat is warm and a perfect fit except it's too long — nearly down to my ankels. It's not a dressy looking coat, I don't feel dressed up pretty in it — but I know it is serviceable. I had sorta hoped to save my money for a kid fur coat, I don't know how much they cost but once I had 62 plus 139 dollars in my bank till I bought My floor waxer and my vaccume cleaner. Oh well, now I've got them and this coat and it will last for years — my lifetime, I suppose. But I don't looked dressed up pretty like I hoped I would. I wish they'd had it shortened before they sent it, now I'll have to find someone who will shorten it. Guess I shouldn't feel the way I do after your trouble in ordering it for me — kid coats never wear well and this one will wear for years — they say they can't wear out and they're much warmer then kid.

Well so be it. A neighbour borrowed our screw driver and didn't return it and now they've moved away. I phoned them at their new house and asked for it and sent Fred to go after it last nite and he didn't get it — the chap had lost it. He said he'd buy us a new one. We'll see. Darn it, I didn't sleep all nite cause of it — the thing costs about $2.98, it was one with different sized screw things — a honey — small but a honey — Fred always loved it. When he said he'd buy us a new one Fred said not to bother. They gave him an old ordinary not different size one instead of our really good one. Darn. I'm so mad I just burnt up and lay awake all night. I hate people who borrow and don't return stuff. They moved away on Sept. 17 and didn't bring it back. We'd never even have gotten this old one if I hadn't phoned.

Well I must have a bath to steam off — I'm so mad. Fred says he'll get it, he'll take back the old one they gave him. He'd better get it, I'm mad. You can't blame me.

Love
Ruby

Oct. 12/51

Dear Kay

Dot Mills and Kath Rogers came over yesterday to see my new coat. They liked it. Dot brought me some cookies. I'm listening to the ball game on the radio now and making grape jelly.

Haven't any news. One nite some time ago I got thinking I'd write a story about Tippy but I just thought about it. Why don't you write about him? Kids would love to hear about Tippy. I can't write but you could. He was so sweet, I wish I could get a dog like him for Billy. Once there was an all black dog who hung around us for over a week that was sorta like Tippy. Bill loved him and called him Boy and he came and went everywhere with Bill. Bill said, "Here, Boy," and he was there. But we didn't keep him. He was bigger then Tippy. We can't have a dog, they're such a bother really. Why Mabel keeps theirs I'll never know — tied up on a clothes line all day. Takes him in and out and ties him in the cellar too. "Such a good home he's got," people say, but that's not a good home to me — tied up, in and out, in and out. Poor dog.

Don't tell anyone but Mable and I went to the library the other day and looked up some of the teacher's salarys in the year book where all the teachers across Canada are registered. Mabel wanted to know what her brother-in-law made — that's what made us go in there — but we couldn't find his. We sure had fun looking up people. That Rose Mercer whose husband left her makes $2300. Stan Martin makes $4700 a year, Al Smith, before he got to be principle made $5000. Ron Mitchel and Jack Dunn make 4700 too. Wouldn't you hate to have your husband's salary so public? Anyone can go into the library and look them up, they're in every library. They use to give them to each teacher but now they have to pay $1 for them. Anyway Janet always wanted to know what made Gwen Martin hold her nose up so high in the air. $4700!! Gosh — I wish Fred got even near that. It's not much for a social climber like Gwen Martin but still it's a lot more than Fred makes — only don't tell anyone.

Kay, don't worry, I'm really getting to love my new coat. I wore it to church and everyone praised it.

Love, Ruby

Oct. 30/51

Dear Kay

Guess what? There's a dame down-hill from us that went to University with you but who she was then I don't know. Hilda Dickson now, married to a Barrie boy in real estate. I tried to find out her maiden name so I could tell you but didn't get very far. Rose Mercer knew her at college too but she forgets. I didn't meet her but she was at Western Alumnae dinner last night. She wore a bunny wrap made like a nightingale and a dress she must have made herself — a green velvet skirt, full all round, with a green brocaded top that looked like drapery material. She's about my size, has a very funny walk, I've seen her walk by here. Rose doesn't think much of her, says she's clever but a snooty type, sometimes friendly and other times not.

Well she said to Fred, "I was in an English class at Toronto University with your wife's sister. Next time she comes here tell her to come to see me." Then she asked "Who did she marry?" Fred said "Dave Graham" and she said "What does he do?" Fred said, "He's a very successful manufacturer. Havne't you heard of Graham's shoes?" And she said oh yes, she had.

She's sort of pretty, pink shiny cheeks. They built a ranch type house last year, cost about $25,000 her husband told Fred, with orange painted doors.

Speaking of orange, I plum forgot Halloween. Wish it were over, it's such a bother, but the children are looking forward to it. Billy wants to be a clown and Sally thought she'd be a horse jockey in my old jhodpairs and riding boots. She looks cute in her jockey hat but my clothes are too big and will look horrid on her.

That dame down hill has such a short waist. She looks as if she has real high high hips starting right under her bust which she hasn't got much of. Mabel said she and Ches always watch her go by and laugh at her funny walk; they think she's trying to walk like a young girl. I'm sure with her high hips she can't help it. Anyway you can visit her next time you come.

Love, Ruby

/ 15

Dear Kay

Guess what? We've bought a new old super dooper piano for $100 and we love it. It's a big huge fancy dancey one marked Cabinet Grand. It must have been extra special in its day. Everyone says it has a lovely tone and we're having fun with it. Fred and I played You'll be Coming Round the Mountain, it's a duet in our beginner's book that we're all practising from. Fred's trying to play cords and octaves, easy but it will take hours of practise to do them natural. The children will take lessons at school in a class, it's cheaper and competition is good for them.

Mabel sold a painting for $25, she's so thrilled. Gee I don't know what I can do. I sure haven't found a talent yet. Today I baked cookies and a squash pie, tomorrow I absolutely must go on a diet. It's going to take me months to get thin, I'm so hippy.

Now about the flanalette nightie you gave me; these cold nites it sure has been wonderful, though two nites ago I must admit I had to take it off it was so hot. But should you want it for your cleaning lady as you planned, I'll part with it though I must tell you I washed it. Oh it was so dirty from being shopworn I had to soap it twice. I never saw such dirt come out of something white. It has gotten a wee bit smaller in size too, I haven't had it on since I washed it, I held it up to me and it's just a 1/2 inch off the floor whereas it used to be dragging. It washed nicely, but Kay, I feel so mean taking it from you when you bought it for Merle. Don't you want it for her even though I've worn it and washed it? I love it on these cold nites. I wish I had it on now, our house is cold, it's just 18 above O outside. Well, Kay, if I keep it please don't buy me a Christmas present — I've had it, see? Please don't buy me anything more.

The children love this cold weather. They go to school to sleighride. There's a beautiful hill there and it's safe and they have a wonderful time. Thanks again and remember no presents for me at Xmas, I'll wear the nightie when I'm home, and we'll all play Xmas carols on your piano that we'll practice on ours.

Love, Ruby

Feb. 28/52

Dear Kay

Isn't mother adorable — imagine buying a new bathing suit at age 71! Isn't she wonderful? Maybe she'll learn to swim. She seems so excited and thrilled in her letter telling me she is going to Florida. She'll have such fun — if only she doesn't get a cold or break a leg or something before she gets started. Gee she'll enjoy it — just what she needs to pep her up. I was so thrilled when Jan wrote and said that the Frasers asked her to go with them and that Oliver was going too. They can play bridge at nite and when the Frasers walk together mother and Oliver can walk arm in arm too. Oh kid, isn't it simply marvellous? Do you think Oliver might marry her? Imagine mother, a bride!!!!

Sally brought me pussy willows last week and they're into pussys. I took them to church for the top of the piano on Sunday and the organist wants me to bring them again. I'd like you to meet her, she has always wanted to write. She can tell a story and really make you laugh. Her husband is a high school teacher, he plays piano and she plays violin and they seem to have such fun together.

Gee I wish I could write. One day I started writing about our old Tippy dog, wrote down all the nice things he did — but that's as far as I got. Right now I'm looking after the Burke's two year old and he's so cute — talks only words and such a pet I love him and he's very happy here without his family. He's been here a week now — I don't know how much longer they'll be away.

I've really been busy. I'm braiding mats these days — went to the library and got books on the Art of Rug Braiding to learn a few pointers. I'm going to practice on smaller ones for scatter mats and when I'm really good at it I'll start making one for our living-room. Save all your old clothes for me, eh? I'm collecting from all my friends and relations — sox, dresses, coats, blankets, anything that will cut into strips for braiding.

Must stop this. I'm having vegetable soup for dinner and it takes so long to peel stuff. I'll put it through the grinder — saves time and tastes just as good — but wouldn't Mother think that was terrible? Not how she makes it.

Love Ruby

Dear Mum

Fred's Aunt Ellen gave Billy an American $1 and he wants me to send it for you to spend for him in the States when you go to Florida. He wants something different but don't go to any trouble hunting for it. He just feels the States is out of this world and whatever would come from there would be more unusual stuff than Canada has. Aunt Ellen gave each of the children a $1. You should see her diamonds — 3 huge ones. She owns 5600 or more acres where she lives out west. She's sitting pretty but certainly doesn't give anything away. She likes bridge so we had Mrs. Stone in to play. Fred seemed to get a kick out of her overnite visit. He keeps saying, "I think she had a good time, don't you?" Why not, say I, she didn't make a bed, didn't dry a dish, she just sat and talked to Fred and drove around with him to see the town.

Yesterday the Burkes left Brice here for 4 hours. Sally had 3 girls in for supper with hot dogs, ice cream and angel cake. This aft Mabel and I are going to see a dame down the street who's keeping house while the Wilsons are away. They'll be back from down south on Sunday and we want to see their huge new house and television before they come back. Aren't we snoopy? But it's fun to see how they live.

Tomorrow I have to go to an old gal's place, Miss Hebblethwaite. She's a retired school teacher from Toronto. We take her to and from church now and then and she's asked me for a cup of tea. she lives all alone way up on the hill near the tower and has lots of money and valuable property but won't sell a bit of it, just skimps and saves — she's a miser.

What color should we paint our rooms? We bought a paint brush today and I'm busting to get going. Kids are snowball fighting. Mine never hit anyone but they're after Arthur.

Have fun on your trip. Sure would like to go with you. Don't bother much about spending Bill's $1, he thinks he can't spend an American $ in Canada and that worries him. Have a good time.

Love
Ruby

Dear Kay

Happy Easter. Aren't the oranges mother sent us from Florida super? And her presents were lovely. We did the jig-saw puzzle right away, glad it wasn't any bigger, it's so hard and long to do with 980 pieces. We had to have 2 card tables set up where they could sit for days and in our little house there's no room. we had to keep shifting them around.

Our livingroom looks so nice painted dove grey with yellow ceiling. It seems to have done magic. If only my braided rug were made it would be beautiful. I can hardly wait for the family to see it. We might paint the kitchen too, things are so wonderful painted.

You should see our cat, he's black and white, just parked here on Good Friday and hasn't left yet. We wonder how long he expects to visit us, he's so at home here Fred's afraid he may stay forever. And we have a frog in our cellar. The kids named him Jewely because Bill says his eyes are just like jewels. The cat wants to eat him.

Sally's having a tooth pulled by a thread — Fred's doing it. Oh it's just hanging there — now it's out!! Hope Fred has a nickel to put under her pillow.

Billy's composing songs for me to have published. I wish some would be really worth while. He's on the student council and is thrilled — got in by 22 votes, even the teacher voted for him, he said. She phoned up and asked herself over for supper again and I had her, it keeps Bill on her good side and she's a bear if he isn't.

Well what I'm really writing you about is your story in Chatalaine. It's lovely, Fred says it's your best. So did Mabel and Chester. I've told lots of people to read it.

Sally's changed her mind about going to camp with Judy this summer. Kids around here are going to camp at Clear Lake and she wants to go with them. I think it's a mistake, Clear Lake has green scum on it and she won't be able to swim in it and the Camp seems so good for nothing, they only run around.

Love

Ruby

Dear Mum

What a gorgeous day! I should go to church. Havne't been there in ages but here's my excuse — Fred goes at l/4 to 10 with the children to teach Sunday School and he doesn't come back till after the church collection is counted and away in the safe. Sometimes it's 1.30 or after 2. If I go to church it means Fred must come to get me after Sunday School and then because he has to wait till after service to count the money Sally and Bill and I have to ask our way home and I hate bumming rides with the neighbours every Sunday. So I stay home.

Last Sunday night Fred and I went to the Pentecostal church. We used to call them the Holy Rollers when we were kids. Remember? Now there's a church with rhythem. Boy! They sure love to sing and clap hands as they sing the hymns. It's really something. The minister likes to work them up and get them excited. Their hymns are all happy, clappy types with easy to catch on to tunes and they sing them right through, all the verses and chorus every time and some times the chorus over and over. You realy want to clap hands or tap your feet if you've any music in you at all because they have a 20 piece band, a Hammond organ and a piano and hymn-sing leader, all whooping it up. The church was really full — much more then our church ever is in the evening — and after the service they all went into a back room for a prayer meeting. I wonder if that is where they roll? The minister said all were welcome but we came home with the Bible student who was responsible for our being there. We met him in Brotherhood Week, he's going through for a minister and is really interesting — his parents were missionaries in Africa and he's been there and around the world twice. He's not the clappy kind but his ideas about religion don't seem right to me. He said they can't have TV or radio or go to shows — but he does go. I said I seemed to be the only one in his church with red earrings — in fact the only one with any earrings and lipstick and he said their women don't wear them in church though they may in other places. Isn't that odd? Sort of deceitful? There are so many things in the world I can't understand — all kinds of religion is one of them.

Love, Ruby

April 26/52

Dear Kay

Our rhubarb's up. I housecleaned the bathroom — now I've the cellar and bathroom done — funny doing bath first but I did the medicine chest and just kept on going.

I met a girl the other night who writes scrips for C.B.C. radio in Toronto. She was hinting for me to tell her how much you got for your magazine articles. I didn't tell her — I didn't know if you'd like it so I didn't say a word. I really don't know what you get anyway — you've never told me. She's the mother of two children boy 8, girl 3. She's a minister's daughter and a banker's wife. Can't remember her name.

I must get going — we ate a chicken last nite — will eat the rest of him at noon. We must have Chester in some day — Mabel's away. I guess I should have asked to look after their cat and dog — they'd be happier here, I bet — always tied up there,

Bev Behrens is having a Stankey product party — sorta like a fuller brush display only the dame who sells shows all her products to those that Bev invites and she gets a silver dish free for having the party. She serves food and the dame sells window cleaner, mops and stuff like that. A nuisance but Bev's nice.

Our radio isn't working well — goes dead — guess a tube is weak. Fred does something then it's ok again. I'm reading sequel to Cheaper by the Dozen. I wouldn't want to have a dozen. Would you?

Jan wrote that you had a good time on your trip She said Dave was tanned and your new clothes are lovely. I'm busting to see them. Fred sold a 5000 last nite. Maybe he'll start getting breaks. A chap promised to phone him today — said he wanted some. Things look brighter. Head office sure didn't brighten his future by offering to take him in there. We'd be farther in the hole and I'd feel terrible wearing your clothes and Jan's in London. Here I don't mind cause people don't know they're yours but in London that's different. We'd have to sell the car to save and be a heap less happy then here. We'll have to change out tacticks and see what becomes of us. The paper said sunny and warmer but so far it's been raining all day. I've a headache — why? I don't know — felt as if I were getting a cold — haven't had a cold all winter.

Love Ruby

Cheaper by the Dozen was an autobiographical book by Frank Gilbreth (1948).

Dear Kay

We had such fun over the weekend when Jan and Harry and the kids were here. Wish you had come too. We had lovely weather cept for one dull day. Jan will tell you about Sunday. It was all Harry's fault. He was stubborn so don't let them blame me that they drove around all day and didn't get anywhere. We went in two cars — Fred and the boys in ours and Harry and Jan and me and the girls in theirs. Harry at the very start of the trip wouldn't say where he'd like to go — just told Fred to lead and he'd follow. He was just like a mule and we coaxed and coaxed him to catch up to Fred and tell him to go to High Falls, no more then a few hundred yards away, but he said no, the kids want to go somewhere else and he wouldn't stop Fred.

Visability was bad so we couldn't see scenery — no distance at all. Harry said he didn't feel like painting anyway. We had quite a time — Jan and Harry arguing and fighting till finally they just quit and forgot about it — but meantime we'd driven over 100 miles. We finally hit the sewage filtration plant and built a fire and ate in the dark. What a picnic! Don't tell them I told you about it or you'll hear it over and over again and it was all because of Harry getting stubborn. Jan agrees.

On Sat. we saw the picture exhibition at the library — it is lovely. I don't think Harry is as good a painter as he was — maybe his painting is OK but the pictures at the library sure don't look like his stuff, I like them much better. With Harry's pictures you have to stand back so far to get what the thing's about. To me he's got the idea that he's so good he can just slap the paint on any which way and it's OK. I can't see it. To me it looks just like paint here and there and maybe it's a tree and sky and rocks and water, you can sort of tell it is, but you have to look a long time to find out or have him point them out to you, I guess they're modern and I'm old fasion.

That tomato butter of Fred's aunt Margaret is awful good. I must let you try it. Fred likes it with everything.

Love, Ruby

Dear Kay

Haven't any news. Thanks for the pictures of cats. Aren't they adorable? I hung them up in the kitchen over the sink. Wish we had a cat, we had a red one for a couple of days and a black kitten came one morning but left by noon.

It's a nasty wet day, rained yesterday too when I went over to see Billy's teacher. I'd talked to her a couple of weeks ago and she said she was disappointed in him so I went to see what he was up to. She says he daydreams, does his work OK but just daydreams. He dreams at home too, thinks all the time and looks far off. But still he seems to know what's cooking. He asks millions of questions, never lets anything go without an answer. He reads the newspaper, sits up and reads it just like Fred, and when he doesn't know what a word means, he asks. I don't know what that teacher expects from a little small kid, only eight. I said to send along some homework with him. He said one day he wished he'd get homework like Sally. Maybe he needs harder work. I don't think he's bad at school, she said he just daydreams. He's going to be a doctor, he says, he's always said that, so he can make lots of money. He wants to make lots of money to go out west to see mountains with snow on top and he wants to ski down them. You'll have to tell him about the mountains you saw in the States.

Kids are going to the farm to visit Mac and Myrtle this weekend. First time they'll be away without one or other of us. We'll see how they like it. Billy might be a worry, he's such a homey kid, won't go anywhere over night alone but he says he'll stay if Sally goes.

We haven't a birthday present for Dave as yet though we did celebrate his birthday. I baked oatmeal cookies, a new recipe for the special day. Must go down street to see what I can get him that he hasn't got — if anything.

Must rush now, Fred will mail this when he goes out if I finish it. This aft I went to a tea — 7 girls — I knitted so it wasn't too wasted.

Love Ruby

Dear Mum

Do you listen to radio programme 50 a Day? It's an Aylmer Soup ad — guess you never do — it comes on at 9.30 over our local station and you have to identify a mystery voice, Please listen to it. The prize money goes up $50 a day till there's a winner. It's worth $500 now. Right now the mystery voice Is Don Wright. I know it. The hints they give are he is from a musical family, won fame at school for his atheletic record breaking — I think they said high jump — and they said he entertained troups during the war, said that others helped to make him famous — that would be his mixed choir — then they said he's known over N.B.C. net work and in the States and on coast to coast net work. Oh it's Don Wright from London I know. Fred sent in ten soup labels for me. If only they'd pick my letter — one in thousands. Please buy a couple of tins of Aylmer's and send them in. You may be lucky. And tell Jan and Kay to do it too. They said his family are in music too and another thing which makes me sure as punch — he was a school teacher. Oh mum, if they'd only pick my letter, $500 would come in so handy. I'm so excited I can hardly write — if only they'd choose my letter or yours or Jan's or Kay's. I've never been so sure of a thing before. Mable's going to send in a couple of labels and she'll give me half, she says. I'm so thrilled. What if I won? I'd buy Fred a new winter coat and a spring hat.

Now I must go, if they pick your letter and it's not right you get $5 If you send in the wrong lable they send you tins of soup. Oh, mum, if I'd only win. Good luck on 50 a Day. I hope you win if I don't.

Sally's making a feeding station for birds. They learnt how at school. She got 77% on her report, Bill passed but he didn't get graded. He's playing over at the school with the kids. Here he comes now. Oh goodie, he says, we're having summer sausage for supper. Wish you were here to eat with us, we're having lemon pie too. MMMMMMM goodbye to my figure.

Love
Ruby

Dear Jan

I'm reading a hot book — Boy!!!!!!! There was a writeup of it in the Globe and Mail that called it the worst of its kind. The Rage to Live by John O'Hara. It's a 50¢ paperback that I bought at the Home and School book sale. Dame said it was terrible and didn't want some kid to buy it so I bought it for Fred for a nickel. He read it — 662 pages — we sure got our money's worth. Has Harry read it or doesn't he read such trash? Hottest book I've ever read — full of sex. Never read such a book. It's in 2 parts and no chapters. Sure holds your interest. If Kay would write fiction anything like this book it sure would sell to the hotstuff readers. I'll bring it home at Xmas if anyone wants to read it. I told Kay it would keep her up nites while she's waiting for Dave to come home from poker games.

Haven't anything else to tell you, it's been rainy and dull all week. I haven't had my nose out the door other then to hang up wash or shake a mop.

Tonite we were asked to go to a dance. $4 a couple. Kath Rogers was having a few couples in before. She got a new black nylon dress for $34 on sale from $47 — a bargain yet she had to pay $4 to have its skirts shortened. We just can't go. Can't afford it and besides the money for a ticket I'd have to get an evening dress — I don't own one that fits me — and then a liquer bottle and a sitter. I'd rather read my hot book. It's more interesting then dancing with Pete Rogers, he's a H of a dancer — worse then Fred by far. Fred doesn't like dances — he says people only go to have an excuse to drink, they never go to a dance until 11 oclock and they stop dancing at 12. That proves it.

I didn't win the $500 for the 50 a Day. Tough, eh? I had the right person but they didn't pick out my letter. Now I think the mystery voice is Mary Martin but I have to wait for more clues. Has Mary Martin lots of relations and 7 sisters?

Love, Ruby

Dec. 13/52

Dear Kay

　　We've talked over electric trains and Fred went to see the $13.95 ones and they're no good, the man said. So we forgot about them until your letter came today. No. Much as we'd like to have one for Billy they are too expensive and we've no place to set it up and leave it set up and there's too much money involved to have it in a box and only out at xmas. No is the solution. Unless we could get a cheaper buy of a good 2nd hand train through the paper we'll forget about it and you all do the same. Thanks for the trouble. Fred too would love a really good train but he'd never let Bill play with an expensive one by himself so what's the sence of teasing him. That's what happens to those good toys, they're too good to let kids play with them alone. No. It was a kind thought but don't buy us a train, please.

　　What do you want for Xmas? Sally doesn't need a sweater now — Jan sent 2 blouses of Judy's and I bought a blazer for $2 at a smoke sale. I wrote mother a list of what we need but I hope you won't spend much money on us. I always feel badly getting so much — I suppose because we need so much. Bill wants a new sleigh, his is worn out, he can't steer it. A sleigh or toboggan would be a good bet — our toboggan has slats out though it still goes. A 3 or 4 seater is best, no big, big job. Anyway don't worry about that. Bill has a Mecano set, also a log cabin outfit that mother gave him, so don't buy either, please. He plays with wee plastic cars I bought him last year, 2 for 15¢, and he has 10 or 12 and loves them best of all. That's all he needs. We have to get him boots and ski pants but those are staple stuff. Please don't let mother buy a lot for us — or you either — it's too hard to shop for so many presents. I wish everyone would forget about it all — only inexpensive things for the kids or they'll get so they want the world with a fence around it. Please just get Fred and me Macleans magazine. Tell Minnie I'm going to make him a catnip mouse.

Love
Ruby

Electric train: A toy train that ran electrically on a track placed on a table.

Jan. 3/53

Dear Kay

Must take down our xmas decorations today. The tree's been down for several days. Blll's playing with his train, Fred's listening to the news and Sally's out for lunch. I love my new garbage can, use it every day. And thanks too for my sweater, isn't it a beauty? For special only. I wore your skirt to Rogers Friday nite, a perfect fit, but I must reduse. We are eating turkey, turkey and more turkey. Maybe today we'll clean it up. We put ours from Mac and Myrtle in a neighbour's locker for a month or two — it's a dark turkey, not nearly as nice as this white one we got free on the ticket Fred won.

Yesterday Bill and Sally went skiing out at the golf club — we took them and wished we were young again — though really that shouldn't stop us. It was mainly Miss Bunt in for supper that kept us from going. We ask her now and then and she always brings us a lb. of candy. She's got one hand off and she's simply wonderful how she gets going and never asks to have any help with her coat, hat, or anything. She lived for years with a girl at the Y and all she ever asked her to do for her in all that time was to close a string of beads.

Haven't any news. We never see Rose Mercer. Fred says she lives up the lake in an old cottage all by herself. I guess she cooked her goose when that roumer of her and that school principle got around. But we like her anyway.

We have Dave's picture up in the livingroom. Mother sent us his ad in the paper so I cut it out and hung him up. The sun's shining, no more snow, Kids go skating at the swamp. Bill brought me pussywillows. Kath Rogers has forsithias in bloom in her house — forced — I could force some too but I haven't a bush.

Here's Billy He says, "Oh goodie, we're having turkey again for supper." Fred loves his tie, you gave him, he's wearing it — it's beautiful, and the sox Jan and Harry gave him are lovely too. Thanks again for everything.

Love— Ruby

Dear Jan

    Gee whizz, kid, I sure was surprised to hear about your operation. I hope you're ok. Where was the lump and what happened? Nobody tells me anything. I've been having a tightness below my chest for ages and now for sure I'll go and have a checkup. I keep putting it off and now it's a little worse since I heard about you. I get terrible attacks of indigestion. Today I have the trots. I must get thinner, and I'll bet for sure I'll have to get specks cause my left eye twitches something awful. I'll let you know what the Dr. says. I've just made an appointment.

    Haven't any news. I've been washing Sally's hair with proxide. I rinse it in vinegar, wash it in Vel. I'm trying everything to keep it fair. I'll only use proxide now and then, lemon once in awhile. It looks right pretty now. Her eyebrows are so shaped and her lashes are so black and curly, she looks kind of cute these days if I have to say so myself. She went skating with higher grades at school — skated with boys. And say, is she getting fussy — won't wear blue pants to match her dress any more cause the boys laugh and tease them should they happen to see their underpants. She'll be 12 next year. I guess I'll soon have to worry.

    Billy came home today and said a kid was going to give him a puppy free when his dog had pups. Bill's so happy. Mary's a hound, brown and black, a gentle, sad-looking dog but very obedient. I don't know when the happy day will arrive. A dog — oh no — what will we do with a dog? I hope Mary's not pregnant.

    The children go skating on the new rink behind the little store down the street it's a honey with two floodlights on it. They want to go at nite but we haven't let them. Maybe I'll go with them some nite, I haven't skated for years and will probably break my coxic.

    Tonite is the Baby Band dance at the golf club — it should be fun but we're not going — $1.25 a person. It would be fun. The Rogers are going, Kath wants us to go I haven't done anything but read and work for a long time. I read a story in Mabel's Ladies Home Journal — My Heart is in Hiding. It was good.

Love, Ruby

Dear Kay

Glad you liked the pants I sent you, we'll celebrate your birthday by baking a cake for the joyful day, Sally wants to make it and I might let her.

There goes that Dickson dame with the high hips that knows you, she has on a green car coat, green shoes, red hat and Plad pants. Looks freeky.

Mother wrote us that you bought yourself a car. A pet. Is it really the smallest kind? Do you feel funny driving such a baby? Now you can come down to see us. We need a new one too, wish we could pick up a good second hand one. Fred's scouting around. I hope he hits a dandy like our old timer, she sure gave us little trouble but is using oil now and Fred's anxious to sell her. Wouldn't it be nifty to have a new car even if it's a second hand job? If only one can trust a car salesman—and they're such a price.

I'm having a bee this aft—6 girls in to cut up rags for my rug. Fun, eh? They suggested it so I'm taking them up on it. Have to give them food but it will be well worth it to get rid of all the stuff I've got in bags upstairs. Must get going, their husbands are dropping them off here at 1 oclock.

I've written 5 letters this morning. I want to write to Over the Teacups in the Star to maybe win $25 but I don't know how to word it. I want to tell about a dame who was vaccuuming with her electrolux, had her budgie flying around the house and the first thing she knew the budgie was sucked up in the vacuum bag. She got him out, dusted him off and put him back in his cage no worse off. It's true. It happened right here in town. I'll split with you, dearie, if you write it up nifty. $25 would come in handy if we'd win.

Mother and Jan were both proud of Dave, both raved and sent clipping from the paper I sent both back so mum could put them in her scrap book. I wish I could do something super to get into her scrap book—you and Dave sure get in plenty.

Sally's nuts about Anne of Green Gables and John loves Lassie that you gave them. They love reading, like you do. Maybe they'll do something famous and get in Mum's book even if I don't, eh?

Love, Ruby

Dear Kay

Today's kid's day at school. They've been taking valentines to school since Wednesday. They don't make them like we did when we were kids but they still get a kick out of the party in their classrooms — they take their own lunch.

We're having company tonite so must get going and clean the house. I'm braiding mats these day so haven't written or done a thing but braid. And read. I'm still at The Walls of Jerico — it's an old book of Kath Rogers. Fred read one on esxuimoes — can't spell esquimoes — Top of the World — in 25¢ edition — it's good, get it for Dave. Fred read it twice. It's a true story about how they live.

Kay, thank Dave for his nice letter, we were certainly thrilled with it. I'm saving it. I show his picture to everyone — this is my brother-in-law. Now with his wonderful performance the other Wednesday I've that much more reason to be showing it off. Mother and Janet told me all about him. Wish we could have heard him — too bad we don't get London on the radio — how thrilled I'd have been to hear him. I'd have asked all my friends in to listen. Mother and Jan are awful proud of him too.

We went to a Community Chest dinner Friday night and had southern fried chicken — man was it good! I could eat a meal like it right now. We heard Rawhide. He use to be in Halifax. He changes his voice and takes parts of dozens of people. He's really clever — Fred never misses his programmes before he goes out on his calls. Rawhide is really a young thing — one wife and one child — so he said. Graduated from Western, comes from London. Has an imaginary spider named Harold that got 70 get-well cards when he was rushed off to Halifax hospital. Harold has all kinds of sweaters and pants and booties and bonnets and stuff sent to him by Rawhide's fans. But Harold — sad to say — died.

Nothing else to write about — but can't waste this space — Thanks for Jack and Jill magazine, it's arriving ok. Sally's thrilled with it.

The Wheatleys we're having in tonight to play bridge. He works in an accounting office — sorta a queer duck, but she's awful nice. Their kids are in Fred's Sunday school class. Fred's still practising the piano — he's teaching himself.

I'd better look at my pie in the oven.

Love, Ruby

Dave played the piano part in Gershwin's *Rhapsody in Blue* with the local symphony orchestra.
Rawhide: Max Fergusson who for many years has had a one-man CBC radio show.

Dear Kay

We just had the doctor for Billy. He's got a temp of 101, not high, but he has tonsilitis. He walks to the bathroom holding his head just so — his glands are swollen and we may have to have them out. We've had 3 doctors say they should come out. This new doc was a teacher then went on to be a doctor, has only practised in town about 3 years; has grey hair and youngish, mild and quiet, yet talkative. I like him a lot. He gave Bill a shot of penisillin or something in his leg and he's off to dreamland now. Should be better tomorrow.

I've been working on rug, have 10 balls of braids now or maybe more. I'm busting to sew it together but the problem is what goes here and what goes next and how many rows of this and how many of that. I guess I'll have fun once I've all the stuff braided together.

Haven't any news — saw a fashion show last nite — makes one feel sorta dowdy seeing such lovely clothes. Sally's getting clothes madness — cried cause she's outgrown her skirts, only 2 fit, the rest are too short. Bill's growing too. We bought him a jacket size 14, it is big for him but Sally can wear it and by next year Bill will be into it better. I have to turn up the cuffs about 1/2 the length of this paper, that's just how much too long the sleeves are.

My daffodils are coming up. Fred's rolling cigarettes and I'm going to have a cup of tea. Have to bake cookies for church group tomorrow. Once a month we're asked to bake 2 dozen cookies, fancy or plain — mine always seem to be plain. I never have nuts or dates etc to make fancy ones. We like your oatmeal recipe. Mind, I love fancy ones too but they cost plenty.

A dame came to the door this morning to sell magazines. I didn't bite, can't buy from every tom dick and harry that comes around. Last week it was the Telie came asking us to subscribe. Send us titles of good books, we have a reading bug, I have one about herring fishermen, interesting and easy to read, nice print and not too long.

Don't tell mother about Billie. She'll be phoning us if you do and there's no need to do that. He's ok, has bad tonsils but who hasn't?

Love Ruby

May 25/53

Dear Jan

Mother phoned yesterday, she didn't read my letter right and thought I said I had a lump. She immediately phoned. I said lungs, a cold in my lungs. She sure can't read my writing.

Got my specks on Tuesday — they seem so strange. I feel he's ruining me. Everything is down hill and I get sick to my stomack wearing them. He told me I'd need glasses all the time in a year and yet I read his finest print perfectly and he said no one had done that in ages.

Sally's class is a choir which is competing in the Kawanis festival. Sally can't sing a note, she's flat as a pancake and I'm so afraid they'll kick her out and she's so thrilled about being in. Tonite they sing at the Home and School Club, Fred and Bill and I will go to hear her, they're showing pictures of Eskimos too. Sally and another boy are the only two who can't sing, she said they're always told to keep quiet. I hope she's allowed to stay in, poor thing.

Russ Jackson called on us Wed. nite — he stayed till 2 oclock and talked about the olden days at home and where's who and what are they doing, etc. I made sangridges, radishes and tea. Being we talked so late I felt we'd talked out so didn't ask him for a meal or to sleep here.

I've been sewing like mad on my rug since you were here and started it for me, have used 4 spools. Can hardly wait to —

Oh here's the telephone truck to fix my clothes line pole, the phone wire runs parallel to it and clothes wind around it on windy days. I get so cross — for 6 years I've had to pick and choose my wash days, can't hang out stuff on windy days at all. Poor chap, it's a cold rainy raw day to fix wires. I'm frozen inside, let alone out. He's getting the ladder out now.

Love, Ruby

P.S. The kitten pictures enclosed are for Minnie, might give her ideas.

July 13/53

Dear Kay

Here's a sumary of what I've been up to. Went to see a dead person Monday aft and to get my glasses changed. Tues. went to a funeral, Wed. morning went on Sally's bike to Miss Hebblethwait's — miser — she was afraid the birds would eat all her sour cherries and asked me to pick them for her and for me. I listened to her troubles and she gave me some African marigolds. Last nite I read — tried out my new glasses that are ok now, needed a different lens and might have ruined me for life. Made Jan's tuna and noodle recipe and a cake. Made jelly out of cherries I picked and had to use coloring to brighten it up — it was so pale because the cherries were too green.

Haven't any news. Sally and Bill are at playground down the street. They do the dishes and off they go. Tell Jan I played her piano book for an hour yesterday — I need practice but the easy pieces make me feel as if I'm super dooper.

Rug is 105 by 80 inches wide. I'll not get at it again till children go back to sehool and the canning's over. Billy has a turtle — Toby — a wee little thing, about 2-1/2 inches long. We're going to put him in a little lake when he grows up. Jan says Judy sold her rat for 25¢ — I never could figure out why she ever bought that rat — such an ugly pink tail — and the smell!!!!!! Sally sold asparagrass and rubarb in May and made 65¢. Too bad they don't last all summer.

Well, I must get going — must make a cover for Sally's comfator that mum gave her — look, she won't part with it — mum gave it to me for the kids to lie on the grass, I covered it and now it needs it again and she wants it redone. She only likes sleeping under it, nothing else. It's all wool and heavy. Remember it? When we were kids it had a higeldy pigeldy quilty sort of cover.

Thanks for the grand weekend and the food you brought, wish you'd come again soon, Fred and the children love having you too.

Love, Ruby

Dear Kay

A truck passed our house and dropped a sack of wheat on the highway last week. I dragged it into the cellar to feed the birds and squirrels this winter but I eat it now and then and it's good for what ails me laxatively. Have a dish of it on the table and I'm chewing it now. I love it. Doubt if the birds will get very much.

Sally's off to camp for a week — she took enough stuff for a month. She sure was happy. Connie, her pal, was in the bunk below. They'll have a hay day. Connie is a tease and happy-go-lucky, our dentist's daughter.

Bill called our cat this morning and he didn't come. Bill was eating breakfast and looked out the window and said There's a dead squirrel over there on the road. And then he said NO, IT'S OUR CAT! He'd been run over and killed. Poor Billy. What will Sally say? We feel badly, he was such a darling, never cried, purred every time you picked him up. Now the mice will come and eat my wheat, so will the squirrels. Beans, I hate animals in the cellar, mice and moles — I wonder if we'll find another cat. This one just came. Poor kitty. How is your Minnie?

Raspberries are nearly over. I had to hunt for the ones I did get. It's not nice picking them any more because there are wee little white jumping things in the bushes that get up your nose.

Did I ever tell you when you go traveling and a skirt or dress is badly crushed just turn on the hot water in the bathroom and steam up the room with your crushed clothes hanging in the steam? It's wonderful. I've a dress steaming now, the bath water's so hot the place looks as if it's on fire.

Haven't any news. I've just been working, played bridge a couple of times. Now I must have a bath, wash my hair, do dishes, berries, pickles, beets, dinner, supper etc, and bed. Each day goes by the same way.

Thank Jan for the beer they left here. Fred and I split the last bottle one nite. Guess we'll have to bury the kitten — a sad affair. I'd rather the Humane Society came and got him, I don't want to bury him in the garden he might be plowed up in the spring.

Love
Ruby

Dear Kay

Haven't any news. I'm making a pickle relish and it's sitting in salt right now, can't do anything with it for a couple of hours so I baked a cake — it's done but too hot to ice, the icing's made too — so all that's left is to write to you and I've nothing to write about. Terrible perdicament, eh? Tomorrow we go dancing in my new little evening dress — not a formal affair but I look super in it I think, and that's half the battle — looking beautiful. Fred's chairing the meeting before the dance, he's thinner and I think it worries him being president of Western Alumnae — this is his first affair.

Now we've had supper — pork and beans, tomatoes, cake and tea. Fred's off to lodge, kids are in bed, cat's asleep. He's cute, a tiger with ring around his neck like a necklace. He's so gentle, I think he's a she. He's a dirty cat, would go to the bathroom anywhere if you didn't catch him. We leave him out all nite — poor thing — but even with sand in a box he prefers the coal bin or my clothes basket with newspaper in it or a rag on the floor — once he went on my bedspread. He's not like that all black kitten; that was the sweetest, he'd be 1/2 grown now if he hadn't been killed. This one, Toots, is a kitten but an old tomcat hangs around at nite, a tiger-alley-cat, a big thing that got Lady into trouble. He likes them young and pretty. I threw my shoe at him and hit him but he still comes around. He's terrible, gives cat yowls, etc. Oh poor little innocent kitty, I'm afraid he'll do her wrong, we shouldn't let her out nites, she's not a fighter, hasn't scratched a soul, never puts her claws out. Such is life — cat life.

My relish is made, I'll give you a couple of jars — nice for hot dogs and hamburgers — lovely yellow with red and green throughout — It's fun having different stuff from one year to the next, I didn't make mustard beans, we're tired of beans.

If you're throwing out pantie girdles, save them for me, I need them.

Love, Ruby

Dear Kay

What a wonderful trip you're planning. I think I'll go down town and get folders on Spain, Austria, etc. so I'll be able to follow you on the maps and imagine what you'll be seeing. How I'd love to have you go to see Abraham, our Egyptian friend, he's captain of his ship, has been all over the world and speaks 7 langridges. He could take you to Egypt on his ship. Gee I wish I had money to go along with you, Abraham would sure give us a good time. Do you remember the picture I showed you of him when he used to visit us during the war — tall and slim and very dark with wavey black hair and a face like the Bible without a beard. His friend Mahammad was in the picture too — the short one in the blazer, drowned in the war. I'm going to write Abraham that you're going to Europe and maybe you two could get together. Oh kid, I wish you could sail on his ship to Alexandria.

I'm sure my pen pal Doreen in England would love to see you too — remember I started writing to her way back in public school and we've kept it up ever since. She is married to a man who works for the goverment and flies to India on business. Looks interesting. Noone has ever called on them for me and heaven knows whether I'll ever see her in my lifetime — though hundreds of letters have passed between us during all the years. I'll write her that you may call her, shall I?

Oh what a wonderful trip. Can I do anything to help before you are off? Where can I write you when you are gone? Have a super dooper time and be careful, don't let them get your money by paying top prices, they say you should bargain. Don't waste time buying presents for us, see all you can, learn all you can and tell us all you can when you come back. Don't worry about sending mail to us, tell mother and Jan to let us know where you are.

Tootsie is lying on the table watching the birds on the patio; she's getting fatter and fatter — Maybe there'll be little tootsies when you come home.

It's near the time of your departure. Happy sailing and good weather — April in Paris — what fun. Oh to be in England now that April's here. I'll write you, bye, and safe journey half way round the world. Lucky you.

Love

Ruby

Apr. 4/54

Dear Kay

Isn't air mail paper thin? If you put this on something dark the writing on the back doesn't show threw and you can read it better. I've got it on top of that beautiful blue table cloth you gave me years ago. Remember?

I've never written a letter to Spain or to Paris. It's fun, I love it. The kids are thrilled with the stamps on your letters — France, Spain, Italy — gosh it's exciting.

All's well with us and the family at home. Sally is almost as tall as I am and Bill is growing like a weed. They like having a paper route — 95 papers. They made $7.54 this week, — if they save they can go to Europe with you on your next trip.

Toots is still without children, she's asleep with a smile on her face, must be dreaming of her happy event. The squirrel has her nest in the bird house again, guess she'll be having a family too in the spring. She stole a scarf, bright pink wool, from a kid who lost it, took it up into the tree and then into the nest with some hanging out of the doorway. It was Jeanie's Xmas scarf and such a pretty salmon pink and fluffy weight wool, lovely for squirrel babies.

I got a perm today — how's you Paris hair-do? I have daffodils blooming in my leaky tub, picked 1/2 a dozen today. They're beautiful but nothing to those in Paris I guess. The librarian here said you'd never be lonely, everyone is so nice and friendly over there. She enjoyed England most of all and you still have that coming. Be sure to call Doreen, they'll come to your hotel or invite you to their huge stone house outside London. Lucky you.

Have fun and don't lose yourself. I thought of you on the 17th of March — St. Patrick's Day — oh to be in Ireland for the Wearing of the Green. But you weren't. You'll soon be home, time sure flies — I'm only on my 4th ball of braid. I'd better hurry or you'll be back before my rug is done. I'll write you again if I find out where in Germany, Switzerland or Holland you are.

Love, Ruby

May 15/54

Dear Kay

Oh our 3 darling kittens — I'll save you one, eh? Wish you were here to choose. One's like Toots and one's a real tiger, and the lady one — Peggy, has a white tip on her tail, one all white left back foot with pink pads and one all grey back foot with black pads. They're so darling. Everyone likes Mike, the tiger best, a honey, grey with big eyes and so lovable. I've been sleeping with the 4 cats the last week. Mike comes up and washes my face every morning. He's so curious and eager and venturous. You'll love him. He's still so tiny, eats only from Toots — the others do too cept once in awhile Peggy drinks milk out of a saucer and eats asparagrass and potatoes.

Sally's at a party and Bill's playing ball, he passed first this time. He brought me marshmarigolds from the swamp on his way home from his paper route. He's awful sweet at times. He brought them cause I've a cold and yesterday he bought me 3¢ worth of black ball candies cause I could suck them and they'd be good for my sore throat, he said.

The kittens are sound asleep. I hope we can bring them home for you to pick out your own. Mother'd have a fit though, woudln't she? But if Toots keeps feeding them and you get home soon all would be well cause they don't go to the bathroom all the time Toots feeds them. Nice, eh? You'd love one of Toot's cats if they're like Toots — she only cries when she wants out and when she wants food she sits up on her hind feet and has a definite pleeding meow not a bit like the one when she asks to go out. She's clean and really housebroken now. Maybe you'd like to have Toots, she's only a year this summer.

The family came during the easter holidays. What fun we had! We missed you but spent hours reading all your letters out loud. Jan read them because she'd read them before and it seemed easier and faster for her to make out your writing. Boy what a trip! Wish I could go. You'll be home in no time, it seems only yesterday when you left. Haven't they pretty stamps in Switzerland?

Have fun and be careful.

Love Ruby

July 9/54

Dear Kay

Steve Master's birthday—guess I'll always remember things that aren't important—haven't seen or heard of my old flame for 20 years. Do you ever see him? Kay, we're so glad you're home again, busting to hear all about your trip. I hope you're not through talking by the time we get there.

Sally passed into Grade 8. She was afraid she'd fail but I'll never know why because she was in the 60% all year. She's out baby sitting from 6 to 9, she gets 75¢ which makes her feel grown-up.

Everyone around here wears shorts. I'm 110 lbs and look horrible in them. Fred says shorts are a thing of the past for me, he fears, so I put them on and go in the back yard where no one will see me, just for a spell to get tanned so I won't be so lilly white in my bathing suit should I go swimming this summer. There are two pigeons who come to our garden in the early morning and around 4 in the afternoon. They scratch up our peas and I should chase them but I like watching them duck their heads.

Haven't any news. Just wrote to let you know we all love you and think of you often. We'll come up to see you but right now traffic is so heavy and we do want to get the upstairs divided into two rooms before it gets cold. The chap wants over $400 to finish it but everyone says Why don't you do it yourselves? Fred's had no experience with hammers and saws. Do you think he could?

Well, dearie, my housekeeping touch is greatly needed on the floors—sure need waxing—glad I stood in line from 5 am until 9 when the polishers went on sale, that was the smartest thing I ever did in my life. I think I'll make a rug for the diningroom—that would hide lots of floor space.

We're still hoping to bring Peggy and Mike home for you to choose from. Peggy loves the bath tub, jumps in to go after drops of water dripping from the taps. Once in she wants out. She's a honey. She has one red toe on each front foot and a white mark on her nose and a red mark on her head.

Must run, Dot Mills may come over this aft, her son takes music lessons near here so she drives him and sits here till he's through.

Love, Ruby

Aug. 22/54

Dear Jan

I'm in a rush but I'll write you while I'm waiting for the washing to dry. Just read your letter out on the old well and found a 4-leaf clover. Here it is. I feel it's a good omen for Dave's new business.

I must clean my house. When I went to the Fair for 4 days I just mopped up and gave it a lick and a promise and I'm ashamed. It really looks terrible. When the neighbours dropped in I really was embarassed by the dust on the floor. We're going to refinish the upstairs ourselves. It worries me but others take on jobs like that and seem to finish up ok. We'll start any day now, maybe tomorrow.

Flo Hunter wrote all their friends and neighbors to come up to their lodge for a week or a few days. Mable came over last nite with her letter — they're not going. She says Flo wants everyone to go up there to buy what is left in the line of food in their store which they have along with the lodge, and to help bring their stuff back to town. Another idea up Flo's sleeve is to sorta obligate us to go there for a paying holiday some time, which in our case she's barking up the wrong tree. Neither Mable or we will be going. We went up one Sunday this summer and Flo had us working all the time we were there cleaning up a cabin, we were there for an hour and a half and we swept and scrubbed all the time.

Tonite we're going to visit a friend on a farm — Iva. She's Chester's sister's son's wife. Only 29, has 3 boys and Mabel says she wants to cry and cry all the time. She's been sick and had an operation for a dropped stomach. She's really a nervice reck. When Chester's sister died she was living with her son and his wife — this Iva — and Iva has never gotten over the shock of her dropping dead. Everything seems wrong to her now yet she won't tell people what's bothering her. She always liked me, Mable said, and her mother-in-law liked me so maybe I can help. How or what I can do or say I don't know but at least I can go to see her and perhaps make her feel better for the length of my visit.

Love, Ruby

Dear Kay

Why don't you write a TV play? You might get a lot of money. I'm thinking and thinking of ideas to write up but haven't hit any as yet. Did you see Nathan Cohen's the other nite? It was so good, simple and funny. He got the title Turning Point late one night while talking to his wife, dashed down to the basement where he works, typed it out and in 3 days he had it written. TV bought it. About a mother-in-law living with her daughter and son-in-law who's just at the turning point of getting a top executive job when his mother-in-law gets bored with life because her hushand's dead and she has nothing to do. She reads a pamphlet about going round the world on $9000 and decides to go but doesn't have enough money, so she goes out at night and holds up movie cashiers and drug clerks every now and then with a toy pistol. All are flabbergasket because of a woman age 55 holding them up — no mask on or anything and she waves them good-by by just dropping her fingers slowly — and they don't catch her. They have in the papers Grandma Bandit Strikes Again. etc The reporter artist draws a picture of her and the son-in-law recognizes her and is afraid to tell his wife — tries to make wife stay home with mother-in-law and not let her out of the house for fear she is caught and will ruin his job. The mother-in-law gets all but $500 and settles for a shorter cruse. The son-in-law tells her he knows and she admits it and tells them why and the son-in-law puts her on the train to Montreal for her trip. He gets rid of her ok but discovers she took her pistol along and tells his wife if she gets any letters from Scotland Yard never to open them. Of course there's detail left out such as the boss having dinner at the young people's house at the beginning of the play and telling the wife her husband's going to be top man and at the end the boss comes for supper the day they send the mother-in-law off on the train and the boss talks about reading in the paper about the bandit striking again and that they caught her. Both nearly die on the spot but he reads on and it says she's an ex-convict who says she got the idea from grandma bandit but they don't believe her.

Now isn't that a simple sorta play — no scenery — just the house and office and the drug store and a movie showing people going in and out. Simple. Oh Kay, with your brain you could write things too — get going — but still, why should you, you don't need the money and you'd

---

Nathan Cohen: A CBC radio literary critic and writer (deceased).

have all that work. But it only took Nathan 3 days to write his. That wouldn't be much time and you could use the money on a trip. Oh so help me, why can't I write? All I think of is things like trying to write or trying to draw but I never know where to begin. I just think about it and never get anywhere. But I'll get at reading and maybe I'll get going at writing. But I'll never be any good.

Love Ruby

July 14/55

Dear Mother

Mabel was afraid to go to Toronto alone and wanted me to go with her by train yesterday so we decided we'd all go to see the Art Galleries, museum, Zoo and radio station and Casa Loma which we did besides eating and seeing the Parliment buildings and Eaton's College Street Store for an hour's shopping—the only holidays we'll be getting this year. Fred and Bill went on the subway while Sally and I bought her a sleevless blouse for 1.98 and ate at the cafeteria in the basement.

At 6 oclock at the Town and Country restaurant we ate all we wanted for $2 and Mable paid for our dinners. We had chicken first then went back for roast beef and all the trimmings—it sure was good. It's a lovely place to eat all you can hold—choice of mashed or fried potatoes, carrots, beans and gravy, all kinds of relishes, celery, olives, pickled crab apples like yours and salads, tuna, lobster, shrimp and Soloman Grundy fish like they make in the Maritimes, sardines, herring, ham, wee little weiners and all kinds of cold cuts, potato salad, tomatoes and cucumbers decorated fancy. You can order beer and wine and drinks but we didn't, the waitress brings you water and bread and butter then you get up and the chef gives you a plate and serves you hot food and you serve yourself the rest. When you're through eating your first plateful you go back and start over again. Deserts are extra and expensive—luscious cakes, tarts, etc. super-looking, but after 2 heaping full plates of food I couldn't eat any or even drink tea. One must go there empty to get the full benefit.

It takes a good hour to eat and one feels just like after a Xmas dinner. Even Sally and Bill ate 2 big plates full, Their noon meal— 75¢—money wasted—it would have been better to starve them till nite. We sure ate and ate, I wish you'd have seen Fred's plate and Mable's, I want to go again.

We sure enjoyed our day. Took the kids to Royal York and Union Station—they really saw Toronto. Only we didn't get them up on top of the highest building or the arena or Eaton's and Simpson's down town— but we really showed Mabel around—I think she had her eyes opened. We should go to Toronto more often.

Love, Ruby

Solomon Grundy: Pickled herring cut in cubes.

Hi Jan

Here are mother and myself sitting. She arrived in perfect time for chicken dinner on Saturday. Yesterday we went for a drive in her car for about 2 hours, then home in time to see the World Series ball game. Ate and watched TV at nite.

We're having a pot roast today before the game — hope all's well — but you know mother. My house has been a mess and men are terrible and the ball game is too slow, no runs, etc. She's settled down now to reading magazines and I hope she stays settled. Everything seemed to be wrong yesterday — she said I wait on Bill too much, Sally doesn't get my attention, etc. etc. Oh my, oh my, life sure was miserable. She'd say — "I do my potatoes this way, steak that, way, and Do this, Do that" — Boy she sure was on the rampage — "Why haven't you this fixed, I'd have had it fixed long ago," etc, etc — "the house is too small for so many people — well it may be ok with only 4 but I couldn't live in such a small place, etc. etc." I wonder if we'll be like that when we're older.

Well that's enough of me crabbing but it sure got me down yesterday — I was glad I said I'd help at Mission Band this aft, but this morning everything is nice and peaceful so I phoned in to say I was staying home today — they won't need me cause it's raining.

Haven't any news — don't know when she's leaving — there's no rush when she's in a good mood but when everything is wrong I'm not happy. Makes me dissatisfied — You haven't this and you haven't that, Why doesn't Fred buy it for you, etc etc — it's hard to take. Well I only have her here once in a blue moon so I guess I should be able to put up with it but my nerves were on edge yesterday and I took it out on Bill and Sally and I had to count ten before I spoke to her. She likes my curtains.

Now I must peal vegetables for dinner tonite and visit with mother. I asked the Rogers over to play bridge with her. Hope all is well.

Love
Ruby

Oct. 18/55

Dear Kay

Today I got a good laugh — I went down the street to Flo's this morning wearing the rosy red sweater you gave me and my grey slacks and I said, "Oh dear, I shouldn't wear this sweater without another over top cause my braiseer underneath seems to make a dint in the sweater right at the most crutial spot, and pulling up my sweater, I showed how my bras was dinted.

Well — quick as a wink Flo lifted up my bras and saw me nude. Imagine! She said, "It really is all you and you do stick out straight." She has always kidded me about sticking out so much and asked if I had faultsies. I never really knew whether she believed me or not. I guess she thought this was her chance to find out if it was me underneath or if it wasn't. She acted so quick and so unexpected that I must have looked shocked.

Her sister said, "Look at Flo, she hasn't anything."

She hasn't either. I guess she just didn't believe anyone could have as much bosom as me and had to look for herself. She must have been quite surprised. Isn't she a riot? I laughed and laughed after — Fred says girls are sure funny.

Our new kitten Susie is getting quite smart — she goes in and out of our milk box now just as if it's her very own door. She jumps on your lap when you say Up Susie-quu, and pat your lap so she knows you want her. Right now she's in the sink helping herself to a drink. This morning she jumped and fell in the bathtub, I had it ready for Bill and she got on the side and she and a towel fell in. She got out in a hurry and sat by the register and washed herself. Oh she's on my shoulders now. She loves to see herself in my new pop-up toaster that mother gave me.

We still are enjoying TV. Sally's been an angel — upstairs to study and very little TV watching. Ohoh here she comes now — and Bill too. Must get going — left-over scollop potatoes and ham from yesterday's supper and tomatoes and cabbage salad with marshmallows and pineapple. Good eh?

Love, Ruby

Dear Mother

Am I ever mad. Last nite Sally baby sat from 6.30 till what was supposed to be 11. The people promised to be home at 11 from having dinner with another family in the apartment across the road. They didn't come home and didn't come home so at 12 Sally phoned them and said I was cross and they said they were sorry. I'm glad she had the nerve to phone them. I won't let her baby sit for them again. Sally keeps her promise and goes at 6.30 so I feel they should do the same and be back when they said they'd be. She's asked to sit on Friday nite at the place where these people were at for dinner last nite. If she sits there and they're late too I'll rave cause the child has to have her sleep. I'm going to phone the woman right now and find out.

I phoned her. I told her if they were going to be late they had better get someone else. She said they were going to a dance and it'd be 1 or 2 so I said I can't have Sally out that late. So she said OK. Gosh you can't blame me. They — those two couples never keep their word and they always come home tight and never when they say they will. So I let her know Sally wasn't sitting till they come home from a dance. I thought it was better to call now then to leave it till later — they've let Sally sit and sit too often. Once it was 3.30 when they came home. I said I was furious about last nite — the people promised to be home at 11 — she said that had nothing to do with her and I said I know I just called to let them know now so they can get someone else Friday nite instead of the last minute. I said after all it's Sally's health I'm considering and I'm sure if she had daughters and they would baby sit she'd appreciate my worrying about Sally. She said yes and we both said good-bye.

Well, it wasn't exactly like that — I was shaking and I'm still shaking but I just felt she should know Sally couldn't baby sit late. So that's that, do you blame me for getting mad at them for not keeping promises? I guess not.

Love
Ruby

Dear Mother

What will I do about Sally — she forgot her box of pens, pencils, crayons, etc on Monday nite. She didn't know if she lost them on the bus, at school or the Y when she went swimming. Now tonite — Wednesday — she's lost them again — either left them in her locker or lost them on the way home from school. This morning she forgot her lunch — it isn't the first time she's forgotten it. Last week it was her new green sweater — it's at Connie Brett's but she still hasn't gone to get it. And you should see how she's recked the $7 case we bought for her books.

She's so hard on things and so careless. I told her tonite she'll have to stay home from the school dance on Friday nite — she's got to learn to be more responsible. This not thinking and not looking after her clothes and things has to stop. She can't go on being so careless. I've got to punish her somehow to make her take care of things. She's so sloppy round here too — never picks up after herself. Bill is different — he tidys up the house if its untidy, but not Sally — and it's usually her stuff that lies around. Really, mother, I don't know what to do — to make her stay home from the dance may help — may not. She said she didn't know if she'd be going anyway. No one has asked her, Connie's going with a boy and the other girls aren't going without one — I guess they just stand around if they haven't boys to take them. I said I never went to a dance without a boy but she says times have changed, girls go stag now. She went Saturday nite to the Y with 3 girls and they walked home and got here at 1/4 to 1. Now I ask you what will she be like when she's older? I didn't stay out to 1/4 to 1, did I when I was 13? Times sure have changed. What does Jan do about Judy?

Well I guess my worries start as the children grow older but this being so careless gets me. I wonder if she'll outgrow it — is it a stage they go thro, or do we parents of today always try to think it's only a stage they're going thro now and they'll improve as time goes on, or are we just kidding ourself and this goes on till they're married? She just seems to be living in a world of her own yet there's no boy friend and she gets good marks in school. But why this forgetfulness? That's what gets me and how to handle it is the question. Have you any suggestions?

Love, Ruby

Dear Mum

A terrible thing. Yesterday at 4 while I was watching Open House on TV I missed an accident at the corner. There was an elderly traffic patrol man watching the kids cross the street morning noon and nite and he had just let a group of children go by, a little girl and her friends were safely across when he motioned that a lady in a car could drive on, but just then the wind blew the hat off the six year old kid and she darted back to get it and was hit by the car. Well the kid was nocked out and she was lying on the road and the kids got her mother and the police came and the ambulance and in the rushing up to the hospital and all, the old traffic man got white as a goast and he had a heart attack and the ambulance came dashing down from the hospital again and took him there but he died on the way.

If they had only taken him too when they took the girl he might still be here. Isn't that sad? Everyone feels so sorry for him but he's gone now. And I missed the hole thing though I did see the ambulance go to the hospital I didn't see it the second time and didn't know till the news was on TV at night about the old man dying. If I had only seen the thing happen I might have thought of the old man and taken him a drink of Scotch or something. Oh dear, I wish I could have helped. The kid is ok, will be up in the hospital for a week but no bones broken and she is fine cept for a lump on her head and a cut forehead — But that poor man was about 70 and doing this patrol job just for something to do and now he's gone forever. I can't stop thinking about him — he was such a darling, everyone loved him. If I'd only asked him here and given him whiskey but I didn't know he was on patrol any more — last time I saw him was at a ball game. Oh, I just can't forget him, I might have helped some way and now it's too late. But I can't be sitting at the window all the time, can I?

We had spare ribs yesterday for dinner and blueberry pie. I hope the blueberries I gave you are ok. I had 2 jars that were bad.

Love Ruby

Dear Mum

I was so mad last nite. We went to the Rogers for bridge and came home at one oclock and here was Sally and her two girl friends waiting for Sandra's brother to call for them. I was cross. She came here Friday too and kept Sally up till one waiting for her brother. I told her this had to stop. Really I can't have that child here like that every time she comes into town. I was mad at her. At her mother, really, because she should be more strick. Sandra's father died and was buried on Monday afternoon and Sandra's mother let her go to a hockey game and a dance on Friday nite — four days later. Both Fred and I felt it was a bit early to go dancing, her dad not even being cold so to speak — he'd hardly have time to be frozen as yet in the ground. And then the mother lets Sandra come here the next nite too to go skating with Sally and Linda. The brother, 16, was suppose to pick her up at 10.30 but he has a girl friend in town and on Friday it was after one when he called and last nite it was even later. When we got home she was still here so we up and drove her right home. Sally stayed here and the brother arrived after we left but it must have been 1.30 by that time. I can't have that sort of thing happening. Do you blame me? Well, I guess you don't.

Bill goes to a skating party tonite — will wear his Roy Roger shirt and his new jeans to match that you gave him. He has his music lesson at noon. He gets up each morning to practise, not much, but he does get up, which is something. If only he'd keep it up so he gets past all the little diddly stuff and gets so he can play carols at Christmas time.

Haven't any news. Sally's trying out for a part in a play at school. Got a letter from Mame yesterday and she said that her sister and brother-in-law said they never saw a child 13 years old with so much personality as Sally has. Nice, eh? Of course the Burkes have always been a blarney kind of family but I still liked to hear it.

Love, Ruby

Jan. 30/56

Dear Jan

Off they go to Sunday School. Bill has a red nose from a cold but not bad. Will you ever get used to Judy going out with boys? Isn't it terrible? Sally went to the school dance on Friday nite with Ted Burrows. He called for her with his dad and mother and at 12 they came here to pick Ted up. Fred asked them in because the kids hadn't arrived as yet — 3 of them — Sally said they brought a girl home with them who lives out the highway where Ted lives and it saved her family a trip into town. On the way to the dance they picked up Harvey Roberts — no privacy for Sally and Ted — a good idea, eh? I don't worry when they go in numbers.

Ted had his pall phone Sally yesterday to see if she was going to the dance at the Y last nite — we had said no to her early in the morning so she went baby-sitting at nite. She felt sorry for herself. I don't know if Ted went without her or not — he hadn't money to take her and hoped she'd be at it with the girls, but Dad and I felt one dance on a weekend was enough. She got her homework done last nite — it doesn't hurt her to baby-sit and study, and doesn't hurt her to only go out one nite a week. When she's older she'll want to go oftener. She's only 13 — we can't let her rush into life too soon. Heavens if they get married at 18 as so many do, it doesn't give them much time to play the field. Gosh, just think in 5 years she might be married. Oh, Jan, doesn't that sound terrible? It makes me so old — a mother-in-law — or maybe even a grandmother — who knows?

Today Bill is having his last day of being 11. Well I guess they have to grow up! Even Susie-cat is getting big. She's not boy crazy yet, she still stays inside and only looks out the window, she hates outdoors and just goes out for her business and jumps in thro the milk box in a flash. She's on the kitchen table with me now — a white ribbon round her neck. I hope she won't have boy friends this spring — but she probly will — that's life.

Love
Ruby

Feb. 5/56

Dear Kay

Fred's working upstairs in Bill's room, Sally is doing homework and Bill is delivering papers — he has 68 and his route is still growing, Sally babysits tonite. She went to a dance at the Y last nite, we were square dancing there so brought her and boy friend home with us — silly to let them walk home when we had an empty car — but she didn't seem to appreciate it.

Bill went skiing this morning at 8.30 and had the TV cameras trail him down the hill taking his picture, he says. Guess it will be on Summing Up, Monday nite. We can hardly wait to see him. Aren't our kids smart? both have been on TV now — though for nothing of importance. Wish the movie hunters would like them for a real movie or something wonderful. Gosh, Sally's girl friend's mother went to a dance last nite and won $50. Nice eh? She's going to New York with it. Fred never takes me to dances.

Well I'd better get going instead of dreaming about things. I'd get at my rug but my sewing machine is broken. Our livingroom clock's broken too and my vacume cleaner broke and we got fined $10 coming home from Mother's birthday party — only don't dare tell mother, she'd feel terrible and send me $10. Don't tell her, please. And my glasses cost $18 for bifocals.

I've made me a cup of tea — such a comfort — especially with a cookie or two. Susie's huddled beside the tea-pot. I must stop writing. I was making up stories all nite and haven't a brain left. I'd like to do something to become famous so I could travel. I've an insurance policy coming due in 1958. I'd like to go to Europe — can I get very far on $1000 and would I have to go alone? I'd get lonesome. I'm sure I'd be a terrible traveller alone. I'd talk about my family and weep. I always get sad and sentimental when I'm alone. Oh well, in 2 years lots can happen — I may never get to Europe. But I'd sure like to see something — even if it's just across Canada or the United States.

Love, Ruby

March 12/56

Dear Kay

Our cat is interested in going out now. Some days she doesn't care and the other days she runs from door to window etc. She got out one morning and played with Burton's tom cat — he must be 10 years old, white and grey and blackish — he's so dirty. He's probably Susy's father. He was Tootsie's husband — Mike and Peggy and Toughie's dad. Anyway we bathed Suzy and she's been inside ever since. Billy used Ivory Snow on her and then put perfume on her and a red and black leather collar that Sally made for a bracelet at camp and it just fits Suzy. She likes it, itches it now and then. The Burton's have another cat too — big, black and white, part Persian named Mr. Britches. A horrid thing.

Suzy drinks tea and likes lettuce. She's really crazy about lettuce and she likes tomatoes and raspberry jelly. She was awful cross yesterday, sat on the living-room window and watched a black squirrel build a nest in our bird house. The squirrel broke off wee branches from our maple tree and took them into the birdhouse all morning and then all afternoon she carried in leaves. I put some dry leaves out from our carrot winter storage but she didn't see them and now the snow we got last nite covered them all up and the sleet this morning really packed them down. I didn't see the squirrel all morning. She was so cute when she looked over the birdhouse yesterday, she looked inside and out to see if it was really storm proof and safe. I hope she comes back to have her family in it. We had so much fun watching the 5 babies one squirrel had in it 3 years ago.

Sally had fun at a dance at the Y with Ted. It's a Y boy's club and the girls were to teach the boys to dance. Ted called for her at 8 with his mother driving them. Friday nite she goes to dance with Bud Nolan, last Friday it was Jack McPherson. She likes no one in particular, thank goodness.

I'm in bed with a cold I can't shake. I've a mustard plaster on me and Fred got me some pills, will be rid of it soon. Fred has a hangover from one he had last week, got rid of his sooner then me. Hope you can read this, writing in bed on my bake board.

Love, Ruby

Dear Kay

I did a painting and sent it to Harry to see what he thought of it. He said it wasn't bad so I guess I'll try again. I only used drawing paper like we had in school when we were kids and Billy's watercolor paints — just cheap stuff that I found out in front of our house a year ago. Harry says I should take drawing lessons at nite school for a year and then painting lessons, I wonder if I'll ever get going on anything special. I've been thinking of writing kid's stories about the squirrel and Suzy and Tippy. Should I write them as a cat or a squirrel, or as me, or what? I'd like to try one like Black Beauty — gee aren't I thinking I'm good to dream I could ever write a story as good as Black Beauty, one of the world's most loved and best seller books?

What are you writing these days? I sent in a couple of things to Over the Tea Cups but haven't heard if it was printed cause we don't get the Star and I haven't had a check sent to me for $25. Boy if I'd win one of those I'd put it in a special bank account for my trip. I guess I should get me a job, Flo Hunter has one.

Did you birds watch Anne of Green Gables on Sunday nite? It was a honey and Caesar and Cleopatra on Monday? We couldn't live without our TV, could you? You feel as if you're out of things without it, everyone talks TV. Only we haven't an aerial but we don't care, we see good stuff and the kids and we get to bed in decent time without one. There's more to see with an aerial but we all might want different stations and then we'd quarrel. This way we have only one for all to look at together.

Must go now and get at braiding or reading. Suzy sends her love to your Willie-cat. Thanks for the Valentines, Sally never writes to thank people — she wrote mother the other day but she never seems to think grownups want letters too. Did Bill ever thank you for his birthday books? I told him to. Many thanks again. Sally's growing so fast, she's into a brown suede jacket I bought before I was married — remember it? And I can get into her shoes — I think modern kids have bigger feet then we did, don't you?

Love
Ruby

Dear Kay

Getting ready for your trip? Lucky you. It won't be long now, wish I were going too. I phoned some gals in the square dancing group this morning and 2 were going away with their families for Easter holidays — one to Richmond, Virginia, and the other to New York — she has relations there and hasn't been in New York for 14 years. Oh to have far-away relations one could visit. By the way are you going to look up Brad Stockton in Paris? I'll send his addresss and oh if you'd only see the Star of Suez docked in England and would run into Abraham — the captain of the Egyptian ship. I wonder if you'd ever have a streak of luck and really be able to see him. It would be a miracle wouldn't it cause London's so big.

I'm learning french vocabularies. Mrs. Bell, Sally's teacher, said not to worry about the accent, she said the french people or any other foreigners don't pronounce English perfectly either yet we can always understand what they say. So from now on I'll get going. Sally's way ahead of me. I've so much to learn it seems impossible to remember everything but I'm still trying.

Here's Suzy, she leaps up onto anything she feels like — no manners at all. This morning I was telephoning in the bedroom and Suzy leaped up on the piano window and pulled down the 2 pots of ivey and all the dirt and one broken pot fell on the coffee table. Lucky it didn't land on those 3 frogs holding arms with a gang of ivy shoots in them. The one pot fell on the floor and didn't break — ground all over everything, I had to clean it up and repot the plants. Well it's one way to get stuff down to make me wash the window. Now Suzy's eating lettuce — her favorite.

No news. I'm trying to cure my constipation, drinking water every time I see the tap.

Love Ruby

Dear Kay

    We went to a dance last nite and what a marvellous success. I won a prize — 3 plates with flowers and birds one above the other on a centre post sort of thing with a handle on top. A honey. Mabel won a straw knitting bag, Dot Mills got a coffee affair and we all got favors at the door — an ash dish with a lady on it wearing a shawl over her head — a silly thing.

    But here's the HIGH LIGHT!!!!!!!. Mrs. Austin, the speaker of the evening!!!! She talked about women and today's a women's world. She was good when she didn't read her speech. She's quite a gal, a writer and a widow who reminded me of Rose Mercer's mother before she went mental. Well, anyway, I went up and asked her if she knew Kay Graham and she said "YES, I know her and I'll never forget her at the Author's meeting in Toronto when she was given her reward." She said this right in front of Mrs. Armitage, a ritzy old dame and Phillis Hallam who's always so snooty. She said — "Kay's speech has always stayed with me." Do you remember it? She said you said it was only now since you won the reward that you really felt you were a writer — up till then you felt people just didn't believe you when you said you were. She said you were a wonderful writer, wrote with so much feeling etc etc. Oh kid, I was proud of you, I was beaming all over with pride and snobby old Phillis was right there taking it all in. And she got really sweet to me — when I asked Mrs. Austin if she knew my old boy-friend Stan Doherty she said Yes, he is in the press gallery at Ottawa and had a baby just recently. I said "Tell him I'm way up on him I've a girl 14 and a boy 12," and then Phillis said,"And they're both real clever children too." Imagine, isn't that wonderful — from her.

    Oh Kay, life's so thrilling at times — having a writer sister sure makes you mighty important in some people's eyes. Oh happy day! I didn't sleep more then 40 winks all nite — thinking how I could become famous like you. I thought I could write about my life but I'd hate to have people reconize themselves, they'd sue me for sure for telling their pasts — all my famous boyfriends — Stan, Herby, and I saw in the paper that Willie Sawn is a lawyer and mayor of Brantford — he used to take me out and Herby wrote poetry about me — now he's on radio and TV. I'd never have the nerve to write about them. Would I?

Love, Ruby

April 17/56

Dear Kay

Oh darling everything is so perfect. I love my jumper you sent me — I have to shorten the skirt but otherwise it fits perfectly. Last nite Fred wore Dave's blue suit to a lodge meeting and he looked so dressed up, it sure is a honey on him and we all love it. Many many many thanks. Bill's happy with his shirt and thanks for the ties, Fred's wearing them tied in different spots if they're worn. Thanks for your yellow dress too.

We've water in the cellar, more then we've ever had. I can't do my washing tomorrow or I might get electricuted with the machine standing in water. I'll house clean the cubby holes in Bill's room instead. Fred's got the room done now all but the painting so I must get his bed back in so life will go on as usual and in a normal way. Bill sleeps in our bed with Fred and he gets in much later then he should. I've been sleeping on the studio couch in the livingroom each nite since Easter and I'm tired of making up the bed and having extra bedding around.

I just washed my hair. Fred dropped a big big drop of white paint on me in Bill's room — my bangs got all wet, and it went on my one eye and my eyelashes were all white — I had quite a time getting the paint off and does my eye ever hurt where I scrubbed it.

Must get Sally to curl my hair. Kids are funny — now she's making sangridges — wasn't hungry when dinner came round and only ate a little, now at 9 oclock she's eating ham, cheese and mustard and lettuce with 2 slices of bread and chocolate milk.

Have fun on your trip. How about buying a sweepstake ticket while you're in Ireland? They say that's the really only way to get one that you know is in the race. Hope you pick us a winner so we can make the trip with you next time. Should you ever see the Star of Suez please ask for Captain Abraham Eveid. He's wonderful.

Love, Ruby

Irish sweepstakes ticket: A popular horse racing lottery in Ireland to make money for Irish hospitals; if you bought a ticket on a winning horse or even on one that ran in the race you might win a fair amount of money.

Dear Kay

I went to the hair dresser last nite and had my hair cut. Really I didn't know that one could get such an uplift from a hair-do. I looked old and kept telling Fred I must go to the doctor. I said I'm looking so old and terribble I think something's down there — a sist, or my stomach or insides have dropped. Anyway nothing hurt me but I didn't like my looks.

But now!!! Do I ever look younger. Really it's unbelievable the change in my looks and my feelings. I should never have let my hair grow. For the public's sake. I must have looked horrid to them. I made an appointment for 2 weeks from today too. I'm not going to neglect myself again. I'm sure everyone thought I was 60 years old. My hair was almost to my shoulders — no not quite — not quite long enough to do up in a bun or anything — just a miserble length. I'm so glad it's cut and I'm young again.

Must get going. I'm making apple sauce with some greenings Fred bought. Haven't had a decent apple or potato this year; our garden is a flop — tomatoes aren't nice, only 2 batches of raspberry jelly, nothing but beets and 2 baskets of tiny onions.

Sally got 26 votes out of 28 to be the atheletic rep in her form, lost only 2 votes — her own and the other girl's best friend's. She must be well liked, eh?

We won't be home for Thanksgiving. We've storms to put up, rosebushes to cover, daffodils to dig up, back yard to fix and trees to trim, so we just can't make it. Sorry, and thanks for asking us.

I might go swimming at the Y tonite. I went all last winter and it was fun but an effort — seems sorta silly swimming in a pool, going round and round, it's so small one's always bumping into people. And being splashed. Woe my new hair-do. Guess I'll stay home.

Love
Ruby

Nov. 25/56

Dear Kay

Guess what? I've got a job — oh kid — I'm so thrilled and so nervice
I don't know what to do. I won't sleep a wink tonite I'll bet. You know
I've been talking about getting a job for so long because Fred wasn't
earning enough and I guess he got sick of hearing about it and he said,
Either do something about it or stop talking about it and I finally got up
enough nerve to go down to the employment office to see what they
could do for me. They asked me all sorts of questions and I said I didn't
really have to have a job but I thought I'd sort of like to have one and I'd
never worked at anything before except a little while in an office before I
was married but it wasn't hard work and I didn't know if I could
remember how to type any more and I thought I'd like to have something
where I could meet people. Well they took down my name and phone
number and said they might call me. And I hardly got home when they
did and I'm to go to Musser's store on Monday afternoon and start
selling gloves. I'm so scared. I'll have to make change and fit people and
be on my feet all those hours — and what will Fred say when he comes
home tonite and I tell him?

Gosh, why did I do it? I could be so comfortable here just watching
TV and working on my rug and I wouldn't need many clothes — this way
if I work I'll have to dress up every afternoon and maybe come home on
the bus or have Fred call for me and I'll always be in a rush with my
housework and have to make dinner at noon. And I won't be home when
the kids get here from school — but that won't hurt them cause they're
big enough now to look after themselves for that length of time — Bill
has his paper route and Sally could get supper. It would be good training.
And I could use the extra money for so many things we need around here
and maybe even save enough to buy a fur jacket and go on a trip — we've
not had a holiday anywhere since we've been married. Besides it's just
from now till Xmas — twenty eight days.

Oh kid, isn't it exciting? I'll be able to buy you Xmas presents for
money this year instead of just giving you pickles and relish. Bill wants a
gear-shift bicycle — though I think he's too young — and Sally wants a
portable phonograph.

Love, Ruby

Dear Kay

I love working. It's so much fun waiting on customers, Such varieties. And I get 20% off on anything I buy at the store. Want anything? What about records or bath towls or what? Sally's going to start working at the store too, on Saturdays. We'll be rich. Isn't it wonderful?

Went to a store Xmas party — super turkey dinner and lots of it. I got a wool scarf made in Belgium, red, white and blue plad, a honey, and a white hankie, nice too, Swiss make.

Haven't all our cards sent out yet. I'm slow. Wish we had the 24th off work so we could go home for Xmas on the 23rd to be out of the rush. I'll ask today, I'm scared but I'll ask. Oh dear me, they're so busy in the stores that last day I doubt if she'd let me go, on the other hand She might so I'd better ask, eh? Bill wants to be home for Xmas morning.

Later — Guess what? I asked off and I can have it. Sally too. We'll be coming home on the 23rd. But not too early. Oh happy day. We can have off. hurrah! Tell everyone we're coming home.

Haven't any news. Here's an article — REDUCING FOR CHRISTMAS FEASTING — when I read it I figured it was just for you — 131 pounds down to 125. Height 5 ft 4 and 3/4. Aren't you about that? Fred says you're taller. I'm about 5'2 with heels and Jan might be 5'4 and 3/4 eh? Fred says not to send it, why worry you?

I tried your bean soup recipe and was it ever good. I'll make it again. Made it one nite when JACK AND THE BEANSTALK was on TV — most aproppriate.

Oh kid, I just ate 4 shortbreads. Are they ever good, far better then last year — oh they are super. Sally has a date to the Y semi-formal. We got 12 outside Xmas tree lights — too few to go on the big tree so we're putting them on the little cedar by the patio. Today a man found a wallet on our counter filled with bills. Yesterday a woman lost her's and an honest lady found it.

Must get going and bake cookies for Xmas concert at church tomorrow nite. What does your Willie-cat want for Xmas? What do you?

Love, Ruby

Dear Kay

We're back in the groove again. Well, not exactly in a normal groove as yet but home and free to come and go as we like until school starts. I've Fred and Bill home in seperate beds for fear they catch each other's germs. Fred has a cold and Bill the 24 hour flue. It hit him bang, poor kid, Boy was he sick — up through the nite I don't know how many times, at least 6. He slept on the studio couch to be nearer the bathroom. The Hade boys are doing his papers, I won't let him out. Me sick? No never — anything like 24 hour flue that might lose me weight I never catch. Fred's reading in bed. He came home from work yesterday and crawled in.

Hasn't it been cold these days and nights? Sally says she freezes, she makes me so cross, she won't wear woollie pants. She'll be sick with a cold too one of these days if she doesn't dress warmer.

Our squirrel friends are so darling. We feed them bread and they're getting quite tame. They try to put a piece of bread they don't eat way up on the branches of the tree, it falls then they come down after it. They keep trying to put it in a crotch and finally end up eating it or burying it in the snow. They look funny hiding it and digging it out. We love them, they look so cute with just their heads sticking out of their birdhouse.

Many many thanks again for the wonderful presents. I couldn't live now without my electric fry-pan and that goes for my steam iron too. I'm sure we'll be ever so much better dressed since we got it — yesterday I pressed nearly everything that we own — it's so easy.

Have to hurry now, Sally wants me to go with her to buy a portable record player. She saved up her baby-sitting and store money for it. I'm not sure whether I'll grow years younger with one around — hearing Elvis Presley, etc — or years older with the racket.

Love
Ruby

Dear Mother

   This is April Fool's Day and no one has fooled anyone around here as yet. Both children are off to school and Fred is just leaving. Today's Bill's music lesson and he's having exams too. He gets me to get him up at 7. Sally just finished her exams and I had to get her up at 6.30. Seems I'm the alarm clock for the family. They ask to be wakened and I'm up to do it. I'm really tired from lack of morning sleep.

   Did I tell you I bought a typewriter? I'm practising daily and the children are using it too. I got it for $95 but it really cost $135. The dame in the store said it was a wonderful buy and I could always sell it at that price or more. I think she was surprised when I wrote out a check for it and took it right home with me. Maybe I shouldn't have spent the money but we've had a wonderful time since we got it.

   Tonite Sally goes to a new club at the Y. She is so thrilled to belong because only a selected group of 20 were asked by the boy's group. She got 2nd highest marks in her room at school and the kid who beat her is going to move out of town. Sally would have gotten more marks only she spells everything wrong like I do. One of the teachers said she always gets the highest mark in the room but only passes 2nd or 3rd because of her spelling mistakes. Tough, eh?

   Bill collected for the paper yesterday aft and an old lady across the road got him in her apartment and whispered to him, "Would you buy me 10¢ worth of black balls?" You remember them — they're real hot inside — all layers in different colours. They're terrible — you get 3 for 1¢. Bill said "30 for 10¢, that's a lot of candy for an old lady, they last about 10 minutes apiece sucking them — they'd last her about 5 hours." Gee I laughed. I wish you could see the little old lady — she looks like a banty chicken. Her husband drinks all the time, he's a house painter. Her brother owns the apartment and they have free rent for the rest of their life the old guy told me one day on the bus — he wanted to be a real pal, asked me if he could come over and talk to my husband but he never came, thank goodness — he's usually tight or having an overhang.

Love, Ruby

Dear Kay

I'm so nervice and excited. Elspeth Montgomery asked me if I wanted to join the Rainbow Ladies Club. It's a ritzy gang of all old dames that meet once a month and have speakers. Every couple of weeks they split into groups — a music group, literary group, art group, and a rug-making group. Elspeth said I'd be for the rug-making group if I'm really invited. It's a Who's Who, Ancestors type of club and they get out a detail credit report on you to see if you're the type to join. They black-ball you if you're not. Oh it's a tough affair. I'm glad you're the shining star in my background that I can boast about. Mind, this doesn't say I'll get in. $3.50 a year and you join only a certain group if they want you. I'll not hear from them till the fall because they stop having meetings in May. Anyway I phoned Alma Reid, another member I know, to see if they really black-ball you and all that dope and she said they only do it in the music group because they have a waiting list to join it and noone wanted this one old dame in, she talks too much and brags about her musical ability etc — so they voted her down. Alma said there are 25 in the group and they meet in the homes and they can't have more in unless someone drops out. They've 7 or 8 different groups, Alma said, but you may never get into any but the rug making one. She said I should feel honored to be invited into it, but as I said, I have to be investigated before I know if I'm going to be a member. They ask you to a meeting when someone can't come, look you over and decide, I suppose, if they'll vote for you or against. So I'm on the list but won't know for months and then maybe never. Well anyway it was nice to nearly be asked and I guess that much honour is something.

I must get dressed now. Bill just came in with 4 kids and Sally's walking up and down like a caged lion with the phone. Breakfast dishes aren't done yet. I was asked to work today but She phoned up and said not to go till Thursday. I was glad — boy after not sleeping all nite from excitement I'd sure short change someone. I was happy she phoned and asked me not to go — if those ritzy Rainbow Club dames know I wear $2.99 Metropolitan store dresses and clerk at Mussers they might not take me in.

Love, Ruby

Metropolitan store: Sold inexpensive general clothing.

Dear Jan

I'm so thrilled — I bought twin sweaters for myself — the most lovely blue and high necked. You can see the colour by looking in the August Lady's Home Journal on page 78. If they'd had bigger sizes I'd have bought you and Kay some too.

Bill's out playing golf and helping the pro shine clubs. Poor mother worries about him carrying his bag. Tell her again he owns a caddy cart so never carries his own bag and at the tournament his chap had a cart and let Bill use it though he was embarassed because all the other caddies carried their player's bags. Bill only got $8, his pall made over 30.

Sally is a keen golfer too though she doesn't belong to the club. She's nuts about playing and wants to join but she's always running around to other things — dance tonite, summer theatre tomorrow, last nite a late movie on TV here. She stayed at Connie's Tues. nite, at Jane's on Mon. after a late drive-in with Jane's parents. She slept till 10.30 this morning. Her business college course is over and she can type 30 words a minute now. Not bad. She caught up and passed the other girls in her class who started a week ahead of her. She said this morning when I spoke to her about helping me clean the house — which by the way, she didn't do — she said she went to business college for me. ME!!!! I said, Don't say you went for me — I didn't learn anything — you're the one who benefited by it, it was just my idea — and a good one too, wasn't it? Fred and I are glad she went even tho it cost us $9. It was well spent and we're sorry it lasted only 3 weeks. However she learnt to type and that's the main thing, she doesn't have to look at the key board for the letters now and a girl can always use typing.

Haven't any news. Sally might wear my new sweaters tonite to the dance but I hope not, it's so hot out and she might be perspirey. Oh, oh, she's getting at the dishes. What's up? She hasn't helped me in ages. Must be because we're letting her go to the dance. I said she couldn't go but Fred weakened and said she could but had to be in by 12. She's not keen on the boy who's taking her so she told him she had to come straight home from it. These kids soon learn all the tricks. Well, I must dry dishes.

Love Ruby

Dear Kay

Jan wrote me yesterday and said your Willie-cat was killed. We're ever so sorry. He was a darling but, Kay, remember there are hundreds more like him and they'd love a nice home like yours to live in, so get another. Variety is the spice of life and cats are so much fun to have cause they're always so different.

I wish you could get one like old Toots, she was such a beauty, a gentle old mother-cat. She slept on top of TV to keep warm, begged for food by sitting up on her hind legs, always came running to the kitchen the minute I started to peel potatoes — she loved the old skins. She was so clean — only we've never yet had one that was trained to go outdoors to dig. We always let them have a box in the house and they always ended up in the insulating sand on top of the furnace just under the cellar steps, and that was their doom. And my end of having cats. I loved them but that was going too far, the odor was too strong. I just can't stand the thought of going through that again and all our cats end up there and I have to clean it up.

Mabel has a cat she never lets anyone see, he's wild when people come, never goes near them. He's scared. Soon as she has someone in the cat goes down cellar. All Mabel's cats have been unfriendly like that. she doesn't like anyone else to pick them up and love them. Poor cats. Poor things. What a life. So cruel, and she thinks they have a good home. Same thing with that dog they had — he loved car rides but they tied him in the cellar when they went. Now do you think that's a dog's life? Poor dog. I don't think Mable was ever meant to be a mother. She never had a baby, tried to adopt one but was never given one. If she can't treat an animal like a human being what would she be like with a child?

Well, dearie, I hope this letter has cheered you up. I don't want you to worry over Willie. There are always more kittens and cats and life is too short. You have to be grown up about these things and take things from day to day. Forget spilt milk and dead cats. Today is a beautiful day, think of tomorrow, don't look back. Can you read my advice? Try it. I live like that. I'm getting too old to think of the past, I don't want to spoil the present with yesterday. Look at the colored leaves outside. Come down and see ours.

Love Ruby

Dear Jan

    This is Sally's first day of cheer leading. It's freezing out. I made her wear her winter coat but at the last minute she only took her car coat so I made her take an old Indian blanket. She took it and was cross about it, but she'll freeze otherwise. I hope she doesn't leave it behind. I feel this cheerleading business is really a cold-catcher but truly she looks so cute in her wee plad pleated skirt and blue sweater and yellow collared blouse and she worked so hard. Boy oh Boy she really practised handsprings and head stands and all the cheer motions. She wanted to be a cheerleader so very much — all but Sally have been on the team before — one gal failed so she wasn't allowed on it this year but all had to try over regardless of being on last year and what jealousy about the position. Sally said what an honour to be on it out of 1000 kids only 8 get on — course of the 1000 who go to B.C.I. all aren't girls — and all don't try out for cheerleading. Anyway she looks awful cute and so do the others.

    Today is the school's first football game at Orillia. If I didn't have to work I'd get Bill and Fred to take me to see it. Bill is on the bantom team and it would give him a good idea what to expect when he has to play.

    You must see Sally in her cheer outfit. You must come for Thanksgiving. We'll be here welcoming you to our humble home, honey, any time, any weekend. Bring sleeping bags if you all come. Bring Mother too. We'll take care of her — she can bring sleeping pills and we can surely control the kids now for quietness. The boys can play parcheesi with her and we can play bridge with her. Don't let her stay home alone.

    Hurrah, hurrah, you're coming, aren't you? Bring Tommie's skates, Judy can go to the dance Sat. nite at the Y with Sally — they wear sweaters and skirts. Bring her slacks too — bring her whole wardrobe. There's a party doll party after the dance. We'll have plenty of room — our bed 2, Bill's bed 2, Sally's bed 2, sleeping bags for Bill and Tommy, cot and mattress 1, studio 2. That's everybody. You'll be surprised at the houses built behind us. Have you seen the new moon?

Love, Ruby

Indian blanket: A light cotton blanket with brightly coloured geometric designs.

Dear Kay

We're putting in the sewer. We can't get a digger so Fred's doing the tunneling himself. It's a slow job — running under the patio from the cellar window by the back steps.

We hope you're coming for Thanksgiving. We're not breaking up tile for the sewer until after, have to have things working while the gang's here. I helped Fred dig yesterday, thought I might lose weight — and too it all helps Fred. He's slow but it's truly hard work. Once it's dug the plumber says he'll have it in in short order for $23. Then there's the kitchen sink to be put in the cellar — it's leaking in spots. And tile to put in the garage and under the cellar floor — we hope that will stop water coming in — we've had trouble ever since the houses were built beside us.

Remember when we first moved here? All the open space? Now you should see it — all built in. Just like a city street behind us, all grown up. Weren't our kids lucky to have the wide open space when they were small and needed it to play cowboys and Indians? Now they don't play like that and we don't mind the houses being here, we like having our neighbours coming here and going there to play bridge. It's so friendly and handy.

Haven't any news 'cept Bill is some sort of representive for his class. He won by 1 point and really was happy. I'm glad he's going into such things, at public school he seemed to always try to get out of them but I think Sally has gotten him interested. She's into everything and loves it — puts her whole sole into things and has Bill doing the same.

I must wash Bill's pants — he owns only 2 pair and they crease so easily, I have to press a pair each day before he goes to school.

Oh I see Marg Hade taking in her garbage cans. I must too. We have to keep the neighbourhood looking tidy so they can sell their house — they're building a new one.

Love
Ruby

Because Ruby's house was in the country it used to have a septic tank but when the city grew around it the urban sewer became available.

Nov. 2/57

Dear Jan

Bill's had his front tooth nocked out and got a hole in his tongue with stitches. It just makes me sick. You know how I've always worried about my kids being hurt and I never encouraged them to be too atheletic so nothing would happen to them but Bill would skate and ski and play rugby and hockey and now his big top front tooth that shows the most is gone forever and there's only a horrid black space there.

It was terrible — he came home about six and he'd been playing hockey and got hit and his tooth nocked out on the ice but he kept right on playing — being brave and spitting blood, I guess, and it didn't seem to hurt much till he got home. Then he couldn't eat and it kept hurting more and more and bleeding like crazy and he spat out the blood or swallowed it and I didn't know what to do because Fred wasn't home. Bill didn't want a doctor because lots of kids get their teeth nocked out and doctors don't fix teeth anyway, but he couldn't get to sleep and so about eleven oclock I decided it wouldn't hurt him to have one of those sleeping pills mother left here for me one time and it would ease the pain and be better for him if he slept. So he took it and got really drouzy but the bleeding didn't stop and then I got scared and thought what if the blood clots in his throat and he's sound asleep and doesn't know it and chokes to death. Oh I felt terrible — so I made coffee and made him drink it and I held his head up and kept patting him and shaking him to keep him awake and when Fred came home we phoned the doctor at nearly one oclock and lucky he'd just come in and wasn't in bed yet so it didn't take long for him to get over here and he looked at Bill and said there was a hole in his tongue that was doing the bleeding and he drove him to the hospital in his car and put stitches in it then brought him home and put him to bed. I'm a reck.

Love
Ruby

Dear Kay

I just phoned the doctor to come to see Bill's tongue. It still has a big hole in it. It didn't seem to heal up the way it should have and I am a bit worried about it cause food could get in it and rot, couldn't it? Poor kid.

I have been going to write you long before this but I just didn't make it with Bill's teeth and cut tongue and the girl at the store being sick and me having to go into work in the mornings and the house so dusty and all. I wrote mother and I guess she told you all about Bill. I just wanted to say many thanks for the food you brought at Thanksgiving and for the fun we all had. It seems so long ago.

A man was to come this morning to do the digging of the sewer but because of the rain and because of another job he won't be here till tomorrow or Saturday. But who would like to dig a hole in the rain and too it is filled up with water. Fred has it syphoning out at the moment but I wonder if it isn't raining in faster then it is going out. I hope not cause it is just about up to the hole in the cellar and it would be terrible if it filled up and flowed over.

Gee talk about worries with kids. I always feared the thought of Bill losing teeth. I guess you shouldn't think of those things cause sure as guns they happen. He looks terrible with his tooth out and he lisps and the other one is all crooked and dead and half broken off. I always have something to worry about. Sally not getting enough sleep and being out late and in case Bill gets hurt playing rugby and hockey — and he did. He's been home a week from school. He has a cold and Sally too and I did but all seem to be better. Definitely I am.

I would like to sell the piano, no one plays it and the piano man said he would give us $75 for it. Now I must give the house a lick and a promise. I haven't anything to write about and I just seem to be writing about nothing. I suppose Mother tells you all I write to her and there wasn't anything else to say except that we spoke to Barney Morris when he was here on Monday nite to speak to the Community Fund campaign. What a speaker — but too fat.

Love, Ruby

Dear Mother

What a mess we're in — mud, mud, mud. The sewer is dug outside now and the plummer is working in the cellar — or was, he's gone at the moment. He's so stupid about things. He was told to do something and I was there when his boss told him how to do it and he did it wrong, so wrong that I fussed and fumed and lost hours of sleep over it and finally they re-routed the pipe. The guy was putting it out the window and that was all right, we told him to put it out the window but where he put it up the wall was the thing that bothered me. Why we'd have had to move the tubs that we intend to get in sooner or later and the new waterpipe that's to go in in the spot where the old one was had to be moved, plus the heavy wiring to it and the water taps and the cord on my washing machine would have had to be lengthened and the light above would have had to be put up for me to see to wash and each time I washed I would have had to run around the furnace to rince from one side to the other cause there wouldn't have been enough space for me to get through. Really, mother, I just had to keep at the guy to make him change that pipe to the other side of the window.

Bill went back to school this week — he still has a hole in his tongue but the doctor said he always would have. As for the tooth, he will have the broken one capped or a faulse one put in, meantime there is only apples that he can't eat and I peal them for him. He looks funny but doesn't complain and he never said a word about it hurting though it must have been really painful.

The rugby season for Bill is over this year, thank goodness. He can do his papers again. All the people were happy to see him, one woman gave him a thirty cent tip. Everyone loves Bill on the rout and all asked him how he was and one dame had to see the hole in his tongue and asked to see his teeth — he sure got sympathy when he collected this weekend.

Sally went to a school costume dance as a brown cat with a red feather cause they were giving all the entrance money to the Community Chest campain with a red feather symble.

Beans, here's the plummer again, I kept putting off going to the bathroom to finish this, now I'm afraid to go for fear he'll hear me.

Love, Ruby

Dear Jan

Bill got up at the School assembly for the first time and read a ski notice to the whole of the Collegiate. He read it real fast yet could be heard at the back of the hall. He read it without taking a breathe and didn't look up to see his audience but he had the nerve to go in front of the whole school and that is something. Not many get a chance to do that and Sally was eager to do it for him but Bill said no, he would do it himself, so he did and even though he was scared and lithped with his tooth out, it did things for him. He would like to take up public speaking at school now. He might be good cause his voice carries well. The thing he had to say he knew off by heart but got too frightened to say it off so he read it. And very fast. The kids laughed but he didn't care, I think he will do it again if he gets the chance. He loves to make people laugh so the laughing didn't bother him and he just went on reading. It took him only a second to do it.

The plummer came yesterday to finish up but the toilet leaked and he made it worse so he will have to come back to fix it and too we haven't the tubs in the cellar yet and there is still the trench to be filled in cause Fred has to tile it so the water will go out under the cellar floor. But you can come any time now, the horrible sewer smell we had is all gone. The cellar is still muddy but Fred thinks he will have all the cementing done by Saturday.

People are buying for Christmas now at the store. Don't buy us anything. Save your money. I think Christmas is a real racket. If you are working in a store you would think too it is a really rat race. The people buy and crab about doing it and they have to give cause the other guy gives and some say they can't afford to give so much yet what can they do when they get so much, etc. It is a lot of fuss for so short a day and so much money is spent. You would be surprised the business that Mussers do and think of all the other stores that do the same.

The TV is talking about aeroplanes, I wonder where Bill is — it's 20 to 6 and it's dark and he seldom stays out late unless he lets me know.

Love Ruby

Nov. 29/57

Dear Jan

I am cross at Sally. She lost her wallet again, student's card, and I don't know what all. She said there wasn't any money in it but she might have said that so I wouldn't get real cross. I told her I refuse to buy her another one. This is the third that I know of. The last one had five dollars of mine in it plus money of her own and bus tickets and a student's card that costs $1.50. She lost a pair of gloves this week too. Really I just give up. Every time I think of her I am going to think of other things. I can't stand it. She never picks up anything after her, she wears stuff and lets it lie where she takes it off and she wears shoes of mine and lets them sit in my bedroom just by the door, never puts them where she found them. I am always picking up after her. I just give up. I bought her a long sleeve sweater for Christmas and I think that is all I am going to get her. For Bill I bought two new shirts and both amounted to the same price. I am going to spend money on myself. I bought me a dressing gown and a nightgown, a slip and two bras and I am going to buy stockings and I might get me a shorty coat at one of the fur sales after Christmas.

The store is getting very busy, I just stand behind the counter and sell gloves, no walking round at all any more. I like it better when we're really busy. They have a phonograph at our counter and all day they play Xmas records and what a noise there is. They have it so loud that the rest of the store can hear and it is really so blasting one can hardly think, yet it gets you and it is surprising how many people gather round the counter to buy gloves. It must be the spirit of Christnas that gets them cause we sold ever so many gloves compared with yesterday,

Look, Flo Hunter was here and she said her sister's boy wants to stop school and work and they can't do anything with him. She said he and his mother were having dinner at a resterant and she lit up a cigarette and he asked her for one and she wouldn't give him any and he said he would buy his own. Flo said he smokes like a chimeney and it is their own fault the way they treat him like a baby but he's so hard to handel her sister hopes she doesn't lose her sanity over him. And I think sometimes like today I have troubles with Sally but mine are nothing compared with other people's, eh?

Love, Ruby

/ 71

Dear Mother

Here I am. At sea! Just like the fish in the picture on this card. What should I do — let Sally wear Flo Hunter's formal dress to the school dance or buy her a new one when the sales are on? Formals cost 29 to 35 dollars and they certainly will be on sale right after New Years for half that. Only the dance is before Christmas.

Flo offered her dress to Sally and had her go over to try it on and sent it home with the jewellery she wears with it too. It's a dark color with a yellow slip under it — a dusty shade that I'd call slime green, dark and greenish looking — pretty with the yellow and it looks very nice on Sally with her light yellowish hair. Flo says it's 10 years old and she wants to wear it herself on New Year's Eve.

I hate to let Sally wear it yet it would save us 1/2 the price of buying her one if we wait till the sales. But would she take care of a formal dress? Her's or Flo's? She lost 2 pairs of gloves last week and two weeks before that she lost one pair. Really, what's one to do? Just bought the 2 pairs 2 weeks ago and both gone in one week. She has one glove of the one pair but both are gone of the other 2 pair. Will she be capable of taking care of a formal? I can't save money by making her one with me working and it would cost $18 anyway and would she like it? She'll need new evening shoes too, her new low heels aren't any good for an evening dress. Maybe I'll buy her new shoes and let her wear Flo's dress and buy her a new dress when they're reduced, eh?

Oh will she be careful of it? That's my worry and problem today.

Love
Ruby

Dec. ?????/57

Dear Kay

They're singing carols on the radio just now which reminds me I don't know what date it is and Xmas will be here before I know it — if I don't sharpen up. Life at our house is sure buzzing. Fred's away on business, Sally is baby-sitting and Bill is watching a hockey game on TV with his boy friends.

What a day at the store! We took in over $500 at our counter alone — for gloves. I've asked to have the 24th off to go home. Fred says it's not like Xmas to go on Xmas Day, half the day's gone before we'd get there, if we drop in at the farm to see Mac and Myrtle, and at the Burkes before we drop in on you.

Let's go ahead with Jan's idea for present giving this year — giving something from ourselves to each other. Is that clear? Have I got it right? I've bought something and wrapped it up for me from you and something for Fred from Dave and you do the same from us and that way we'll all have just what we want and not waste money and you'll be surprised when you see what you're giving me and I'll be surprised when I see what I'm giving you — specially because it will probably cost about ten times as much as anything I could afford to give you.

It's not fair that you should buy presents for our children and not get something sorta on the side but you mayn't spent a lot on them cause I can't spend a lot on you cause we just bought Sally a $35 dress — formal — and shoes, and for Bill skiis for $25 and he has to have a ski jacket. If you really must buy him something he needs a cheap plastic raincoat that folds into a small parcel. He doesn't need golf balls — has hundreds that he's found on the course. Has my clubs, has ski poles. How about sun glasses — there's something he'd like — for skiing in a storm. You've seen colored ones in pictures in magazines. Yes. That's just the thing, but don't spend more then $2.

Wait till you see Sally's hair cut — no more pony tail. It will be quite a shock to you,

Love Ruby

Jan 6/58

Dear Mum

Today I went down to the unemployment and put in my request to go on unemployment pay — silly of me not to when I can get $9 a week until I get called back to work again. The only thing is I have to go down street every Monday morning at 9.30. But it's worth it. I've already spent my first $9 on birthday presents for Sally and Bill. A Bible each, a jacket for Bill and a dress for Sally. I bought pencils too — there's never a pencil here when I want one. I tried on 2 dresses but they were too tight. I really am not in shape to buy one — too fat from the Xmas eating.

It's snowing — Bill will be happy. I'm sitting by the fire in the livingroom watching TV special news — the Russians are really going ahead. I hate to think of what they could do to us. I have to think of other things or I get scared. You should see our new salt and peppers — 33¢ each and are they ever honeys. They really are sprinklers for wash or perfume; they've screw-on plastic tops and you can squeeze them to get pepper and salt out. We had to make the holes bigger with a nail or a meat squeere and they're the only 2 they had or I'd have bought everyone a pair. They're about 6 inches tall, nice size so you don't have to keep filling and filling them up and you can see how low the salt's getting in them cause the light goes through. Oh they're super, no corks, no rust. They're perfect. I love them. Wait till you see them.

Fred went up north with another agent and did fairly well. They split the commission. We bought Fred a new coat, a Harris tweed, brownish with a new fuzzy hat — sorta fur felt. He wasn't sure he liked it but I do. It's got a flat crown — not a high thing like his usual hats and it really is good cause his head doesn't look so long and narrow. Clothes help; he sold a policy.

Now I must get supper. Don't know yet what I'll have but there's plenty of stuff around. I haven't the nerve to write to Jan — Sally and Bill left their car coats there — Oh oh oh Jan will have a fit. I hope they come to see us soon — I hate to have her mail the coats to us — such a bother. Why are kids so forgetful?

Love
Ruby

Dear Mother

I just came back from the Unemployment Office after collecting my $9. Honestly it's not like relief or getting something for nothing and losing one's self respect, like you said. I pay in to the unemployment fund at the store — it's taken right off my pay and we pay taxes too so it's only right and what's coming to me in a way. I can use the money and I might as well have it as not. True I do have to stand in line and wait my turn but if you're buying tickets for a hockey game you have to stand in line too so what's the difference? Fred drives me down when he goes to work and I do my grocery shopping after so it isn't time wasted and gives me an outing in the weeks when I'm not working. As for Fred feeling his neck about taking me down there, that's up to him. Only he knows if he's working as hard as he possibly could and selling as much as he ought to.

We took the Hade kids and Bill out to ski. He loves his new Jacket, a red one just like the other skiers. We got him hockey pants too, they are such funny things on him but he had to have them, he was the only one without pants on the team.

Chester went to Toronto to get his mother yesterday. She has cancer of the lungs but thinks it's pheumonia. The doctor said she has only two weeks or two months to live. I don't know where they will bury her, Toronto or here if she dies here. I must get Mable to give me a perm, my hair is so straight that my hat looks awful. This aft I'm going over there to quilt — Mable's having quilts for a bedspread. I will never get my rug done if I don't soon stop running around. I was going like a house on fire for awhile but all I did last week was cut up stuff. It isn't hard work, mum, I love it and if I had a room to leave my stuff in I think I would go in the rug making business and sell them, I love to do them so much.

Had four ladies in yesterday — just asked them at noon and gave them store cookies. I should have gone to a church group but don't think I'll join this year — nothing but baking, meetings and washing dishes. They're having a turkey dinner, serving 600 people. That means baking 4 pies and serving all nite. I don't feel like doing it. Do you blame me?

Love, Ruby

Dear Mum

Happy day, I put the last braid round my livingroom rug. It's done and it's already half worn out in the middle. It's taken me about 5 years to really finish it but it is well worth it, I think.

I was out for a cup or tea this aft at Mrs. Easton's — only me — and we had a nice visit till her son came home and I had to play checkers with him. I was so mad sitting there playing checkers with that kid when I should have been home getting supper because Fred is going to lodge tonite and is stepping up — 3 more years and he will be Head Master. Sally goes to Hi Y and Bill to a Red Cross meeting that is good for him. He'll learn how to take care of anyone who gets hurt skiing and all free and he will find out if he would realy like to be a doctor as he always says he would.

I haven't my glasses on and I am typing this with my eyes shut, I can't see a thing close up without my glasses. I don't use the typewriter as much as I should simply because it's in the bedroom and not handy to get at.

Right now the phone rang for Fred and the door knocked — Connie for Sally — and a couple seconds later Gary came for Bill.

Rogers had their dog killed yesterday cause he has been sick since November and was getting worse. He had little use of his legs and kept falling down and Kath was afraid that he would lose control of his bowles and she would really have trouble so they had him killed. He had pheumonia and something that young dogs get that is fatel — not distemper but something like that. Anyway it is better, I told them, to get rid of him. Sound's cruel but it was crueler to see him suffer and he whined and shook and shivered so and couldn't clime up on chairs and things cause his legs were paralyzed. Poor dog. But he is out of his suffering now. Kath use to get up in the nite and lie on the chesterfield with him and take him out at two and four in the morning. she works in the afternoon too and can't stay up all nite with a sick dog. She misses him but will get over it, the house will be cleaner and they won't be eating dog hairs any more.

That's all the news.

Love, Ruby

Head Master: Of the Masonic Lodge.

Dear Jan

Here I sit — I've been lazy all day getting hot flashes again and I just go nuts — now why should I be hot? I just had the front and back doors wide open for the last 10 minutes and as soon as I shut them and sit down to write you I burst into flames. What a heat on my forehead. I could fry an egg.

Probably because I am having a tea tomorrow. I invited everyone on the street and I'm weary thinking about food tho all I'm giving them is sangriges and bought cookies but I'm wondering if it is too big a tea and I should bake a cake. I'm having it so all the neighbours can meet Marg Jones, the new girl next door to Allen's. She's young but still someone has to introduce her to the neighbourhood so I guess I elected myself. Some can't come — Helen may come later but at present she's busy — so she says. Thelma who I was at 2 weeks ago had her mother taken to hospital and she was told her mother night die anytime so she'll come if she has enough nerve — she's quite shaken up by the shock. Chester's mother may not come with so many people and her lungs; Sue Allan, who I wanted specially to meet Marg cause she has Rolf 4 and Marg has Linda 4, said she wouldn't be going out on account of the new baby. Her mother has been staying with her since it came a month ago and everyone is thinking she is a willie-nilly and a silly little sap that she can't look after herself. It is only this week that the mother has been going home to sleep at nite and the dad brings her over at 8 in the morning. He is on pention and goes home and comes back here for meals and takes Rolf to nursery school and home again goes home at nite to sleep alone — tho I think this Monday the mother ackshally went with him to do his washing. Everyone thinks Sue's husband is foolish to put up with such baby stuff. She's perfectly healthy but when the baby was coming she was scared to move. Poor girl — she's an only child and her mother's a boss.

Now I'll buzz off. I'm taking my nerve medicine again to stop this heat. Dr. says heat's from nerves. I'll see. Life is strange for we girls. Whenever I seem to take life easy I get flashes. I guess I should work hard all the time. No rest for the wicket.

Love, Ruby

Dear Jan

Well I guess my tea was a success. 10 came. I didn't visit much with the girls — served all the time and that new girl's kid, Linda, is one HECK. She threw cars — plastic ones of Bill's I got out for her and Mable's niece to play with — she banged on the piano and kept closing and opening the lid with bangs. I was having a fit. She got into my cupboards and the bathtub and ate all the pepperment candies. Really she had me a reck. She threw things down the cold air vent. I was scared she'd nock dishes off the what-not and I've all my good stuff up there. I was afraid she'd break all Bill's cars too. Mabel's niece was so good I just could have eat her. You know how some kids are, you would just love to keep them. Well Mabel's niece is just that type — a clever kid if I've ever seen one — talks sense at 5 — but that Linda never said a sensible thing.

Everyone was nice to Marg, asked her to come to see them — just how sincere I'm not sure after the way her kid acted. Anyway I'll not offer to baby-sit. I had enough heaving off of things. She's too much of a handful. Hope they don't live near us too long — yet Marg's nice and friendly and asked me over. I'd better be thankful for small mercies — that Linda's the only one she's got.

From now on my dining-room rug comes first. I must settle down, I've so many things to do — cupboards need housecleaning and painting — I always marvel at you getting yours done at this time of year. Mine go for years it seems before I get up there to do them. I'm not like you, I work like a feen one day, next day I'm dog tired. Now I think I'll get going. I must get at rug today. Nothing like working — wish I had someone to give me a push when I get lazy. I really love to be lazy.

I read the Nun's Story — what a story — is it really true? I wouldn't want to be a nun. Boy are they ever under control. Sure wish I could disoplin myself like that, I would be spelling every word right and typeing without a mistake — never would I let an uncorrect letter pass out of my sight like I am going to do with this one. Bye now, forgive me for doing so.

Love, Ruby

The Nun's Story: Book by Kathryn Hulme.

Jan 28/58

Dear Mum

I must practise typeing cause today I was offered a typing job when I went down to collect my $9 at the unemployment and I didn't take it because I was afraid I might get to be a nervice reck. I wonder if I should have tried it. They said they would give me a free training course but it was full time and Fred has always said he doesn't want me to go to work all day. I guess I should get out the typewriting book and practise letter writing. Nice of the unemployment to ask me if I would like a typing job, eh? and if I would like to take a refresher course that the unemployment give for old girls like me. I asked if I would change my mind would it be ok to let her know and she said yes, any time. She sure is nice to me.

Gee if I would be able to spell and type better I would have tried that job. Fred definitely doesn't want me to take it, he says I would worry and then get sick and there would be doctor's bills to pay and the kids would suffer with me being crabby. They like me better this way—fat and jolly—ohoh fat—but not jolly. They said I looked like someone in a circus tonite, I washed my hair and kept putting my hand through it and it was standing up strate and I look like a mop.

Tomorrow I'm really going to reduce, says me—after eating a spoonful of orange marmalade—boy how I like that rind. Sally says I look like a cillinder—round and no curves good for the new style clothes—but I mustn't say that. Spring's in the air and I have to get thin to get into my clothes that I have. I don't want to buy any new ones now cause I hate to buy a size 16 when I should be a 14. Oh dash I'll really try but I'm always starved before I start and I keep saying, oh I'll eat this today cause tomorrow I'll really start dieting and each day I eat and eat.

But think, I could have had a fulltime office job—should I have taken it? Fred says NO. But did I miss the boat? Oh I wonder if I should have tried it. I'm sure I would have worried but it would have been better pay then the store—oh woe—if they only hadn't offered it to me my mind would be in one peace.

Love Ruby

/ 79

Dear Mum

I've made up my mind. I am not going on a diet cause the more I say I am the more I eat so I am just going to eat and be fat. I try to eat less and I starve myself then the next meal I eat twice as much so that is the reason I am giving up the idea. I'll just eat less and not worry about being fat or not eating this and that. I am just going to enjoy life and eat without thinking of getting thin.

It's snowing. Happy Bill for his 14th birthday. The ski magazine is coming ok, thanks, and he loves it — dreams of all those wonderful looking ski hills, wishing he'd live near them. He's just nuts about skiing, just nuts about it, goes to ski school every Saturday morning and to the Ski Club Saturday afternoon. They say it's good and safe when they learn right — so don't worry.

He's having a birthday party — 6 boys. He's a bit embarassed about having it yet he wants one. He says "Guess this is the last one," but he said that last year. He really loves to have parties for boys. Rob Rogers wants him to go to his house for a party on Sat. nite with girls but Bill's not interested, only goes to please Rob — if he goes at all. I'm not rushing him. He isn't girl crazy, talks to them if they phone him but he doesn't phone them. He still is a KID. He built a snow fort at the back of the house. He doesn't want to stop playing — making forts, skating, hockey, kid's stuff. Skiing he loves best. Wish he were as keen on his school work. The Lion's Club here are helping the students who are really good to go through college if they haven't money. It's nice for the really energetic students, the principal helps pick the worthy ones for a helping hand. Bill and Sally want to go to college but we will see. Sally doesn't know what she will do, she just wants to go to college and I am saving money to have her go if she's good enough. She thinks she got 70% on her last report. Bill doesn't know what he got but he found out that knowing the vocabulary in french isn't enough. He just got a pass in it, so Sally is helping his with the grammar part — he was quite surprised that there was more to it than just words. He'll learn.

Love, Ruby

Dear Jan

The unemployment phoned and asked if I'd go to work at the Shop and Save store for sales and I said I'd think it over, I phoned Rosie Cram — she worked there and she said don't go, the manager's terrible — has a bad reputation with the sales girls. I phoned back and told them I didn't want to go cause Mussers were going to call me in in a month's time and I've worked there 2 years — so they said, oh no, you wouldn't want to work there — so I didn't go. The unemployment dame sure is nice to me. You can refuse jobs 3 times and then they take you off unemployment — so here I am still collecting and waiting to be called in to work. The way there is nothing doing at the store I'll not be called in for ages — people just don't have the money to spend. Sure wish there wasn't such unemployment — makes me worry — Fred finds it tough selling insurance. He needs more sales to make the convention — poor soul — I'd hate his job — perswading people to buy what they won't beneifit by till they're dead.

Bill gets his picture taken today for the school paper. He wore his blue jacket that Kay bought him and it's short in the sleeves now. I hope he keeps growing, I want him to be tall, not short like Fred and me. I hope he remembers to keep his mouth shut, he looks terrible with his tooth still out and he lisps and the other tooth is all crooked and dead and half broken off. I was always afraid of Bill losing his teeth. I guess you shouldn't think of those things cause sure as guns then they happen.

I hope Harry's cough is better. I sure know how he feels not getting sleep for I went through nights of little of it myself when Bill was at his worst with the hole in his tongue, though he suffered in silence for fear he'd have me crying for him. Poor guy, but we have so much to be thankful for cause he could have been so much worse. This way time will heal all.

Love, Ruby

Dear Kay

Sally said this morning what she wants more then anything in the world is to go to a boarding school and then go to Europe at the end of her grade 13. Her German teacher is keen on her eagerness and suggests that she write you about trips for students etc. Find out about the school Mary's daughter is at — get much much dope on things for us. Please don't say we haven't the money — we'll do our best to get it — borrow on insurance — anything to help her if she's serious. I'd like her to go to Europe — Grade 13 is only 2 years away — it isn't too early to think about things. One has to plan — who will she go to Europe with etc. I've saved up so far $1,782.02 in the bank. So I have a start for her. She has a policy of her own and one we have on her. Gee I hope she can get there, she's so keen. Her German teacher said no jobs were available — not to go with the thought of staying to get a job — there aren't any.

Bill wants to go too — simply to ski. He wants you to bring him ski boots from Switzerland. He'd pay you for them when you come back, he's so ski-minded.

Oh, kid, do you think Sally will really get to Europe in two years? She'll be 18 then. Is 18 too young? What's best for her? I had this idea — Grade 13 then teacher's college, then Europe. Then she'd have something to fall back on — the way she wants it — Europe, then college and what? Well two years is a long way off but we must plan and save for it. She's so anxious to go — has an Irish teacher going back to Ireland at the end of school term who has asked her to visit them in Ireland. I have such wonderful dreams of her going abroad. I'd rather she'd go then me. I'll be content to see your pictures of it.

In 22 days Sally will be 16 — time sure flies. It's hard to believe I've a 16 year old daughter and a 14 year old son. I don't feel a day older but I must look it. I'm raring to go this morning. It's Sally's eagerness to go travelling that's got me ambitious. I feel as if I could do anything.

I must clean the house now and dream about Sally's journey through life. Will she really go — what's ahead for her — ambition or just thoughts????

Love
Ruby

Feb. 6/58

Dear Jan

Good thing I have one sister who writes me cause Kay only writes in a blue moon. I wish you would ask her to find out about that school in Switzerland where Canadians go. I showed her the newspaper with pictures about it when she was here. I guess I'll have to forfite my trip to Europe so Sally can go. Her German teacher wants her to write the United Nations ambassador for information. I really should look into things; grade 13 comes so soon. Gee she might meet up with a statesman. Elspeth Montgomery says it pays a dad to send his daughter to university just to catch a brainy man. Get the dope on Mary Atkin's to see what her kid's doing over in Switzerland, etc. Sally is keen but she's not a brain. She got an average of 73 — everyone failed in math but 4 out of 40 and Sally was one of the 4.

Gee I'll have to get a full time job with all these expensive ideas floating around and now Bill wants to get going and study so he can go too. Woe is me, my insurance policy will be gone — no trip for me — but then they're young and life gets tougher for them to get ahead, and me, I'm old and can be happy with little — a cup of tea, TV and some food and I'm happy. (Fire trucks just dashed by.)

How I'd love to send both to Europe but I can't go if they go cause I've no money for 3 and even getting money for a (more fire trucks, chief, etc.) trip will be plenty without a year at school over there. But plans are cheap and it's fun — your star hangs low if you think and talk about it but if you don't it's high and too far away to reach — let her talk and plan — seems those are the ones who get places — look at Kay and Dave — I think I'll get the TV woman to come to see my rug and get me on her program and maybe people will get me to make rugs for Sally's fare over (one truck's gone back) my dining room's a mess, all over the floor are piles of material — I must get cracking.

Oh kid, I wish we had money to give them their wishes. I wish I were a brain so I could make money to give them their heart's desires — not candy, shows, etc. but education desires. Gee I'm not going to spend a cent — no clothes, I'll wear all my old stuff — I'm going to penny pinch from now on. Wish I'd saved more all thro life.

Love Ruby

Feb. 9/58

Dear Jan

You're right I'm not spending money on the kids. I'm mad at everyone. In one of those blue moods — no one cares about me or likes me — ever get in that mood? Bill says I baby him and Sally never picks up a thing, her room's always a mess. She drops curlers in bathroom and never picks them up. I'm fed up. She stays out every Friday and Saturday till one or after. I get sick of it. I feel she needs more sleep, she works all Saturday at the store and goes to Sunday School at 9:30 till after church, never sleeps in.

Bill's as bad — stayed up Friday nite to see a late movie and then got up at 8 to go skiing. Home for lunch and out skiing at the club by 1 oclock, home for supper and out skating at nite or watching TV till after the news and even the wrestling after that. Fred never says BOO. I fuss and fume about them not getting enough sleep — I wear myself out yelling at them — so now I'm not talking or doing a thing for either one of them.

And do you know what? I didn't mention it before but for Xmas Sally gave me a $3. hair dressing ticket at *her* hair dressers with the thought I'm sure that she'd use it if I didn't. Fred didn't buy me a thing, nor did Bill — he bought Dad a $13.95 brief case but nothing for me. What a sucker I am, eh? Time I woke up. The thing to do is let them do as they please and never say a mean or bossy word and you get a smile and you're a swell guy. Well that's it. You clean house, get meals on time or they crab, make beds, mend, wash and iron and press pants every day and what thanks do you get? NONE!

I'm not going to give Sally my money to go to Europe. She puts every cent she earns in the bank — she'll have an insurance policy paid up by the time she's 19. Bill has one he's paying for too. Let them look after themselves from now on. I'm thro saving for them, they don't care for me. Guess I'll end up dying with what I've saved cause no one wants to go to Europe with me — look at Kay — she was going to go to Europe with me in two years time but there wasn't a word said when I told her I had the money — guess I'll go by myself when I feel like it. Now I have to go to the unemployment to collect — wish I were working so I could get more money to travel. Don't work too hard, you never get any thanks for it — least I don't from my 3.

Love
Ruby

Dear Mother,

Now Sally doesn't want to go to Europe till she's older cause her German teacher said she'd get more out of it. She's too young, he says. She's talking of going to teacher's college again — so she's not sure just what she wants as yet. Last nite it was a new boy from Orilia who brought her home from a Y dance — Murray is in the background it seems. Friday nite it was Don Reid. She's happy and that's all that matters and what fun she's having at her age. She cheered at a basketball game then went to a school dance after — Bill sold cokes at it and we went square dancing.

Sally had to go to Sunday School meeting this aft. She's in too many things, I think. She sure doesn't study as much as Judy does — she gets a fair mark and as long as she's getting in the 70s and stays there I'm not hoping for scholarships. She's happy and trying and keen on life and she's getting lots out of it and that's all that matters. Teachers think she's ok so we don't worry. She's normal. Bill's slower but he discovered he wasn't studying enough to get good marks and is trying harder now for his next report. But don't expect them to get marks like Judy's. Kids are all different and we wouldn't want them all alike. As long as they're doing well and are happy that's the main thing.

One thing for sure. Sally will never be a clerk in a store for the rest of her life. She's bored and hates it. I've no idea what she'll be. I only hope she doesn't think she's in love and get married young before she really has something to fall back on. School teaching or something. Bill's too young to worry about — in Grade 9 they don't know what they want. Grade 11 they have to start thinking about things. Only 2 more years high school for Sally — boy, don't they grow up fast? I'll soon be 50 and how I remember when you were that age. We sure have the years slip by in a hurry — yet as each day passes you never think about time passing and just go on in the sane old way.

Now I must stop. I'd have typed this for you but I'm listening to a sermon on the radio.

Love, Ruby

Feb. 12/58

Dear Jan

I haven't Valentines for everyone — sort of silly sending them, don't you think? At our age? Who cares? Even the kids don't, they're growing past it. Here's one for you to give Harry, I gave it to Fred last year and saved it so now you can use it for Harry. I've one for you to give him on Father's day too if I don't forget to mail it to you when that time comes. And here's one Valentine for Tommie and one for Judy — I'll not sign them then you can let them send them to someone else next year — gee how tight can one get, eh?

Fred bought me tulips — pink with white edges — beautiful, 5 for 59¢ at the A & P. Got them yesterday and took me to church turkey dinner last nite — cherry pie, turnips, potatoes, dressing, and I had 2 helpings of turkey — was it ever good. Hmmmmmmmmmmmmmm. Men's Club put it on. First time I've eaten a served-to-me dinner at the church.

How's your diet? Lost any weight? I'm cutting down but not last nite — $2.25 for the two of us — I ate up our money's worth. Today I'll try to eat less. I'm not sure if I've lost but I feel more ambishious.

Do you watch Open House on TV? They have a famous painter on it telling people how to do it every Friday. The first lesson he said to get a crayon pencil and lots of big pieces of paper and draw in bold strokes anything you see — not hard stuff — just apples, oranges, vases bottles — stuff like that — but do it in big style and practice that. Don't be afraid. Look at an apple then draw looking at the paper, don't keep your eye on the article — so I'm trying to draw as he said. I think it will be fun. I use wrapping paper to draw on — free hand — he said throw everything you draw away but draw and draw and don't be afraid. He says people are afraid and draw little and not free. Next lesson is Friday, try it, kid. Women have better color ideas then men, he said, but men have better structure. See these drawings of my tulips Fred brought me? I should have drawn them each day so I'd have had the practise of the bud stage. They really opened up a lot today. One tulip has 9 petals, boy are they pretty. I wish I could give everyone a bouquet like them.

Love, Ruby

Feb. 13/58

Dear Jan

I have to go to the dentist on Thurs. aft. I hope to get home in time to see Open House. If not will you watch to see what the artist tells you to draw then tell me. Chester took a picture with his colored camera; he put it on the wall and left it there so I could sketch it. The picture was in black and white with beautiful shadows from the sun. Really lovely. I can't draw it as it really is but this is an idea. Get it?

Thank Judy for her nice letter — I can't get mine to write letters — too much on the go and I have to get at them and at them. I made pancakes for Bill for breakfast, fish for dinner. We bought Bill new boots and goloshes for Sally. Bill skis all Saturdays and Sundays, you should see his tan — really red but it will tan. He loves it. They found a wild bees' nest and ate the honey but two dames came today and took it and are they ever mad. They all went to the tree and ate the stuff — the bees are sleeping now — can't sting.

It's 8 above zero. I'm hot, next minute I'm cold. Someone from Toronto sent Sally a Valentine in the mail today. It's taped and big — I'd sure like to open it — who in Toronto knows her? I've never heard her say she knew someone there and it's dated and mailed on the 12th. I'll tell you later if we find out who it's from. But she keeps secrets.

How's everyone there. I just found out I had $100 less in the bank than I thought. Oh, kid, I wish we had money. How about sending Judy here this summer, they can go to business college in mornings for $3 a week and get a job in the aft. I could look after Tommie when you go to the convention — I'll be working only in the afternoons and surely he'd be ok playing at the supervised park playgrounds behind the store. Bill will be here, playing golf and Tom could go with him. I want Bill to go to business college to take typing too — it's good for them.

Happy birthday to Judy — tell her to save the $2 for Europe. Put it in the bank for a trip, I just saw a Buick pass with lots of silver — I bet it was like Dave's — what a masterpiece — it must be a beauty to ride in. Happy birthday, have fun. Here comes the gang for dinner.

Love, Ruby

Feb. 14/58

Dear Kay

Guess what? We've the cutest cocker spaniel puppy playing ball on piles and piles of paper in the kitchen. Cute! You never saw the like — black with spotted legs and chest and stomach, housebroken in a fashion and good and quiet — not a peek out of him — or her — all nite.

No, we're not keeping him. He was run over in front of the house so I had to bring him in and up to now noone has claimed it. We'll watch for an ad in the paper. It is a honey but not for us — Bill says, "I'd like him if he were clean," Sally says, "I'd like him if he were a cat." Fred's the only one who likes dogs and he doesn't want one. Period. Bill was here alone with him last nite and wiped up 3 wet spots and that was that as far as he's concerned. I don't have to worry about Please can't we have a dog? from now on. Wonderful, eh?

Are you nearly frozen? It's 8 above zero. I went down to the unemployment this morning, too many called to collect and they ran out of money and had to go to the bank to get more. Now we're only to come every other week so people who come late won't have to stand outside in the cold.

We named the dog Valentine because it's Valentine's Day — Val for short. He's curled up like a dog, now, asleep on the papers. The man thought he'd killed it, it was so still, so I said put him inside our fence and I'll call the Humane Society but I didn't cause he came too and is ok and I want to see ads in the paper and give him to Rogers if no one claims him. Kath said to bring him over tonite. He has an all black roof in his mouth and is so quiet — they'll love him. Their dog Molly was rough and chewed everything, this one sleeps most of the time, you'd never know he's here except to hear his feet on the floor or a slight hoo-oo once in awhile. He's breathing heavy now — he may not be feeling too well as yet — maybe he's snoring. They sure smell up a house like a dog. I'm glad no one here wants to keep him. People next door have a collie pup; I went over one morning for coffee. She's lonesome but I can't go running back and forth. I must get going — my beds are not made.

Love, Ruby

Feb. 18/58

Dear Mother

Don't worry, I'm not working too hard on my rug, I don't work on it steady, I never work on it at night and I haven't enough stuff to really finish it anyway. I sewed the braids I had and I got it humpy and I was so mad that I haven't ripped it as yet. I said to Fred this is the last I'm going to do, I'm getting sick of it.

Sally went to a school skating party last night and won a spot prize of a $2 certificate from a ready-to-wear store. They know what they do when they give those $2 prizes, the things they sell are all more then that and to make use of the prize they have to spend more; she wants a sweater that costs $13 she said this morning — see how they get the kids?

Sally is going out with different boys — not the same one. She still is friends with Murray, still goes out with him, but she doesn't go steady — they say there's a difference — she cheer leads tonight. I must go to see her cheer lead one of these nites — she does a flip with Connie while the others do splits and a star jump — whatever that is — I have only seen her practice at home but never have I seen her do a flip — our livingroom is too small for it — it's a complete turnover she says — do you get me? I'm not sure if I do either.

Bill didn't go to the skating party because of his ski first-aid lesson. He is really interested in the course and it is good for him. He didn't take part in the week-end ski meet, he isn't that good. Don't worry, he doesn't jump he just likes to ski.

Haven't any more to write about — you can tell Kay I wrote a story about our squirrels but I can't find the first part. Fred doesn't encourage me — I guess he doesn't think I'm any good, but at least I try and I keep sketching things too in bold strokes like the man said on TV, to get the fear feeling out of your system. He said to buy 12 tubes of oil paints and 5 brushes, palette knife and linseed oil and turpentine. It should only cost $12 to get all you need for beginning. But I don't know if I'll be good enough to invest that much. Anyway I'll keep on drawing — all I need for that is a crayon and paper. It's fun, mum, why don't you try it?

Love
Ruby

Dear Mum

Fred's boss bought a poodle dog for $85 and now he's sick with the disease that Roger's year old pup had, his legs paralyzed and he suffered and shivered and shook. No fun having a sick dog around. The collie pup next door is a lady dog. I don't like having dogs around, wish they didn't have him, they always go in other people's yards and in our garden — though their's hasn't come in ours yet so I might be counting my chickens before they're hatched — but dogs do use the neighbour's yards for their dirt — never their own yards. A dog from the apartment comes over here regularly and I chase him whenever I see him.

The squirrels aren't in their house. Mrs. Squirrel had a fight with her skinny husband yesterday — he chased her and they both fell from the tree. They got up and ran up the tree again — neither were hurt. I had fun watching them. Mrs. wouldn't let him in the house but he got in anyway and you should have seen the birdhouse rock — she soon chased him out and he kept trying to get in. Once she tried to get a crust of bread in the door and she couldn't, She dropped it cause Mr. Squirrel was after her. She scolded and scolded and then they made up and sat beside each other on different limbs for awhile, then the mother went up the tree and he ran after her, she jumped from our tree to his tree and off they went down it and up the street out of sight. Today they're not around.

Boy it's cold outside, I hate going out in the cold. Ding — I got a hot flash again, didn't before Xmas until January, now I get so hot I cook at times — I'm taking nerve medicine and maybe that will stop it. I took 3 bottles at Xmas, Dr. says that should stop it. I'm ok constipationally, no pills — I've been having success. I'm happy about that, I always had to take a laxative every day. Chester's mother is still here still alive — she's looking fine though she breathes heavy and her skin's getting saggy and yellow but she never complains. I hope I live to 100. I want to see how this world makes out with rockets and moons and all. Hope you do too, mum, you've still got lots of pep.

Love
Ruby

Dear Kay

Haven't much to say but the Bell Telephone got after us yesterday for talking so long on the phone. I was guilty. Kath Rogers phoned me and chatted away til a man asked us to let him use the phone. We got off like a flash and next day they phoned me about curtesy on the phone. I apologized and said it was my fault etc etc but I had 2 teenagers and one specially was on the phone a lot so I asked if he'd speak to Sally and tell her the rules. I felt it might do the trick cause she never listens to Fred and me when I tell her to get off the line. She was really afraid — she told her boy friend last nite she couldn't talk to him very long cause the operator even knew her name and I told her the second offense they take the phone out and she really believed me. I imagine they would too.

I expected the guy on our party line would sooner or later complain about us but I didn't think he'd be using it in an afternoon — I'm usually at work then but now I'm not and Kath phones me around three every day. I don't know who the party line is, I didn't ask the operator. Maybe I should have apologized to him but I would have been too scared cause he might be awful mad at us. Anyway if it cures Sally it's worth the complaint.

Last nite there was a big write-up in our paper on how to beautify your home with a braided mat and it gave all directions to make them and said one 9 x 12 is worth $500. Kid, I guess I've made a fortune, mine is 10 x 13.

I'm almost afraid to use the phone now but I called Dot Mills to see how her kid's mumps were — her boy wrote us the cutest letter with a drawing of a bear with mumps and said I hope you don't get the mumps cause if you do you'll look like this — his drawing was far better then mine — more mumpsy. I've been drawing all day — just for fun.

I'm reading the Bible — I've never read it — the one I'm reading isn't the really one, just a pocket edition — much easier reading and it gives you the story in a much simpler form. Fred's read both and says you really learn by reading the pocket one, the other's too long and too hard to understand. Sally is reading the really one — reads some every nite in bed — but she doesn't get much out of it.

Love Ruby

Dear Jan

Fred helped me perm my back ends. I'm sitting with a towel round my head for 30 minutes. Hope it turns out ok, I didn't waste much time doing it — still have half a bottle left over in case it's no good, I'll get Sally to do the ends that didn't take. She's studying now, says she wants to hang around here this summer so she can play golf. Gosh she's not anxious to work by the sound of things. I don't know what she wants to do — says she hates clerking. I can't afford to let her play all summer. She'll have to work for a living. I'm not going to work all day and let her play golf and have boys around. She doesn't want to go to a summer resort as a waitress — says they have to work too hard — up at 5 and they're so tired by nite they go to bed early and don't have any fun. She doesn't want to do that. And I don't blame her.

She cheered at Orillia and stayed for a dance after — 4 girls and a bus load of boys — What fun, eh? Next week she goes to B.C.I.'s formal — she just has one grand time. Today she took $5 of mine to buy a new sweater. I don't know what she thinks we're made of. I'm not buying her everything she wants, she can spend her own money same as Bill does. Boy were we ever born 30 years too soon, eh?

I bought me a new dress — a $24.95 one for $9. Now I've got to get thin so I can look nice in it, my arms are too fat and it's a sleeveless sheath with jacket, wee bow under bosom, with or without belt, but I'm too busty without it. Sally likes it off me and Fred likes it but thinks it's really a type for skinny bosoms. But ding it, I love it — it's so petite looking and I do feel thin in the skirt. I've so little to wear — everything I have is so old. The one you gave me makes me so old and matronly looking, Fred said, "No wonder Jan gave you that." He didn't blame Harry for not liking it on you. I wear it to work where Fred doesn't see me in it. If you want it back I'd be glad to send it.

Oh I wish I could lose 6 lbs. I'm trying will power but I'm starved now. I might eat an apple — did you try the cottage cheese diet and fruit? That's a fast way to reduce if you like cottage cheese — 1-1/2 lbs of cheese a day and fruit. Should lose 5 lbs in 3 days, they say. But I'm not that fond of Cottage cheese.

Love Ruby

Feb. 27/58

Dear Jan

Guess what? I think I bought that dress too small for me. Last nite I took it in an inch on hips and all round and Sally wore it for the 1st time in its life. I was going to wear it to Mable's but Sally said what should she wear, she was going out with Don Reid to a Y Club party and Don's president and they were going to his house to eat after so she wanted to look special, though she just bought a pink sweater that cost her $7.98. Why for $1 more she could have bought a dress exactly like mine for herself and really had something worth $24.95 — though perhaps they only put high prices on the tickets for a sale so you think you're getting a bargain. Do you think? Anyway it's cute and I like it for only $9. It's a honey on Sally. I'm wondering if it's too young for me. It would be nice if I could wear her size and she could wear mine. I'd hate to see her as fat as me but maybe we could hit a happy medium. If she'd grow a bit taller so she could hold extra weight and I'd get thinner — well — well — oh my diet — I tried yesterday to eat less and I starved and I had indigestion at nite and I got up and ate 4 pieces of bread and butter and then I got to sleep. I'm sure not going to do that again.

Here is a sketch I made through our kitchen window — actually the apartment should be a double job but I didn't seem to get it just right — but it was fun doing it — my first street scene. I've a headache and my stomack's upset. Sally has been saucy. I told her to wash her own sweaters — she was so sweety pie to me last nite when I loaned her my dress and now she's so mean. Gosh she makes me mad. I never do anything right for her cept wash and — no not iron — I never do her blouses right — but I notice she never irons them herself. She never does dishes, once in a blue moon she makes her bed and tidies her room — but it's always, "Do this for me, mum," "do that for me, mum." Oh these kids! I'm going to look after myself — no one else will. I must take an aspirin for my head.

Love, Ruby

Dear Kay

It's snowing — just gorgeous. I've putted around all day, ironed, mended, cleaned and swept our sidewalk and neighbour's on each side of us. I took a Reader's Digest to Sue Allen and swept my way over and back, just as I was going in the house our new neighbour Marg asked me over for a cup of coffee so I swept my way over, had coffee and swept my way home again.

Bill is going on a ski week-end tonite with a busload of skiers to Lake Placid, N.Y. He paid for it out of his paper route money. I hope he has fun, he needs a pick-up like this. Sally goes everywhere and he sits here. I've a chicken in the oven, I want him to have a good meal before he leaves cause if I can feed him in his excitement he'll not be so nervice on the way. I packed all his things in Fred's roomy old Gladstone bag, he'll have less trouble finding things in it. If only he's safe and goes to bed early, that will be my worry till he comes home on Sunday.

The chicken smells good. I feel starved. I'm so fat. I oiled my head — my perm that Dad gave me was a fizzle — I put olive oil on my head and hot towls, now it's soft and greecey — it will have to take its time to get the greece out but it was so dry and horrid all week. Sally's hair-do she got down town wasn't nice either — too old looking and all waves on top of her head, made her head big and heavy looking. I didn't like it, nor did she — she won't say so but I think she likes a pony tail best and is letting it grow again. Her hair's really dark now — too bad, I like her a blond but nature will be nature.

Wed. nite I went to an Eastern Star tea at Kath's sister Millie. They want me to join. Do you think I should? Would I like it? They meet twice a month but you don't have to go every time. $10 to join and $4 a year and odd times you have to take sangridges etc. Kath says it's wonderful belonging, they're so friendly and when she was sick she had so many cards and flowers and people came to see her, she says just for that alone it's worth it. What do you say — join or not?????

Love, Ruby

Eastern Star: An organization of women whose husbands were members of the Masonic Lodge.

March 5/58

Dear Mum

Bill's home from his ski weekend. He had a wonderful time — tired but he'll get pepped up with a good nite's sleep. Boy I'm weary, I may sleep this aft. We went out playing bridge last nite — wore my new petite dress and liked it but I sure can't take late nites — 2 oclock is too late for me. Fred's off and I've my dishes done, I think I'll go back to bed now and sleep, it's that kind of day, dull and damp and cold.

About the Eastern Star, I don't want to join it really but I don't belong to a thing and I wonder if that is good for me. I am so lazy that at nite I don't want to do anything but just sit and watch TV or read or go to bed or have company when I feel like it. I think I will wait to join it when I am older but when I still have Sally and Bill home I think I'll stay here with them.

My squirrel's building a nest — there she goes with old leaves in her mouth. Yesterday she took ever so many loads of old bark off our tree into the birdhouse. She's out after more — I must feed the birds — they're looking for something. I bought Schneider's brounschwager sausage on Sat., was it ever good. I was hungry for it and I got some Alpine cheese — much like limburger — with Caraway seed in it — it was good too but Fred doesn't like limburger so I had to eat it myself.

Sally's home now — talk, talk, talk, she'll be 16 tomorrow — remember when she and Judy used to push each other around in those little wicker doll buggies you bought them? She wants to drive the car now, wants a temperary license. Doesn't want to wait till next fall to learn at school, wants to get it tomorrow. She's so happy — some kid wrote a poem about her and some other kid wrote a piece of music about her and a teacher who goes square dancing with us called her Our Sally — They all seem so fond of her.

Haven't any news — I smell like limberger. I wanted to ask you about something that happened long ago — now I've forgotten what it was. Did you and Daddy ever square dance? But that wasn't the question.

Love
Ruby

Dear Mum

Sally is in a fashion show for teenagers on the 20th of this month — I wish you could come to see her. She is modeling coats and jackets — she is too small and only wears a size five, she said. There isn't much she can wear because she is too flat chested and short. Poor kid is sorta disappointed she isn't chestier. I told her she isn't eating enough, I'd be thin too if I ate only the things she eats. I can't get into anything of mine in the skirt line unless I put an extension on it with safety pins and there are two dresses that I wear to work that I can't even get into at all so if I get called back to work I don't know what I'll wear. I made a cake and we ate it all but four pieces, it had a whipped cream icing and we had cheese and crackers at four — no wonder.

I guess we'll eat fish tonite. Kids like fish. They are taking their lunch to school again instead of buying it. Bill wants to save money. He never asks us for money — not even for bus tickets, Sally is always asking. She never has any money — but you know why — she puts everything in the bank. Fred put in $23 for her yesterday. Bill is saving his money too since the trip to Lake Placid. He sure enjoyed that trip. It was good for him, I notice the grownupness of him since he came back. He likes skiing and the gang that ski are really nice, there aren't many and they get to know everyone so well.

Haven't any news. I never go out. But I never care. I'm a really stick-in-the-mud. I've been drinking too much tea. Yesterday I had so many hot flashes — I wonder if it's from drinking so much tea. I read that the reason women are so crabby is they have too much water in their system. Yesterday I sat around and had about 10 flashes — today I washed and worked hard and I only had two. Just goes to show you shouldn't be lazy. Work's the thing to keep them away.

There's a funny looking kid going by the house and he's talking to himself — I guess kids all talk to themselves — there goes another one with a paper bag. Sally's eating a peanut butter sangridge and she left the jar open — oh does it smell super — gee I love peanut butter — oh I only ate 1 apple, 2 pieces of bread with butter and honey, 1 egg and a slice of bacon for breakfast, and cup after cup of tea with milk and no sugar. I'm starving. Must get dinner.

Love
Ruby

Mar. 7/58

Dear Jan

Fred is out working, Bill is doing homework and Sally is talking on the phone. I am waiting for some ice cream to freeze. Kay sent me her diet and I guess I will have to try it as soon as Fred buys me some grapefruit — gee it's tough getting fat — so hard to lose.

Chester took his mother to Toronto. She seems in good shape except for tightness in her chest and tired all the time. I must write to her. It may be the last time I'll see her, you can't tell with cancer of the lungs — she may go quickly. Anyway a letter now and then wouldn't hurt me for no matter how well she is now, she may not have many days left in this world. She has a great old memory, reads a lot and hasn't too many friends left at 83.

Good for Tommy wanting to go in the public speaking contest again — that gives him confidence and I sure would incurage him all I could cause the first thing we know he might be a member of parliment or he might like to do speaking jobs like a lawyer, etc. Bill still wants to be a doctor and is he ever studying harder since he got that low report. He's really trying now and doesn't hurry down to see TV, he is saving his money too since the trip to N.Y.

Haven't any news. Mrs. Clark gave Sally a mauve tulip for her birthday and a lot of stuff — an orange, banana and apple and an ice cream powder, potato chips and candy, artificial cigarettes, marshmallows and cookies. She came up for a cup of tea. Our milkman had a son on 3rd of March — Fred has him insured so we gave him a flannelett sheet for a present — not much — just a sheet to hold the baby in while burping. The baby's name is Harold Hans.

I braided today — I'll do more tomorrow. It's fun to see the stuff go down. But where to put the braids???? Bill suggested the bathtub. I don't know what I'd do without TV and radio — I love to braid and listen to CBC Matinee — they read part of a book each afternoon and each 15 minutes is different — discussing this and that and telling you what's in the news, spring fashions, kid's education, etc — it's really interesting and the time sure goes fast.

Here's Dad, must get dinner. Bill will come soon. Help Tommy with his speech he may be a politition when he gets big — he seems to like talking.

Love, Ruby

Mar. 8/58

Dear Jan

    You should get mother interested in drawing—who knows we might have another Moses. Would you like one of my pictures? Not an original exactly but a copy to a degree of Earl Bailey's Xmas card. Could I be fined for copying a perfessional? I didn't make it just so, you'd hardly reconize it as the real thing so maybe it isn't illegal. I sketch all the time—the artist on TV said to draw and draw and then when you aren't afraid to draw to buy oils and paint. So I go around sketching the buildings I see through my windows and kid's faces and copying things and drawing vases and apples and anything that I find and feel like drawing. I like to do scenes and buildings and portraits best—it sure is fun. I doubt if I will be a Rembrant or have my paintings hanging in people's houses, I may not even get oils or paint at all—just keep on sketching. Fred doesn't encourage me with anything I do, not even rug-making—only me working for money seems worth while to him. I guess business is tough with all the people out of work and it sure must be discouraging to him. He never objects now to me working.

    Here is my latest masterpiece—a copy of the picture over the chesterfield but done from the spot in front of the register from the floor angle. How do you like it? Does Harry think I am improving and is there any hope? Do you think I should keep on trying? Mother encourages me but no one else does except Chester who is no better then I am. I must get out and do the real stuff and not the copying of things but it is so easy to copy cause it is too cold to go out and too I am doing it for the practice of depth, etc.

    Haven't any-news—I am so hot at the moment that I must go out to cool off. My glasses are steamed up from the heat of me—boy oh boy—I must be 95 degrees in the shade at the moment. I washed 10 sweaters and Bill's ski jacket this morning—how that guy loves skiing—tell mother don't worry he's no jumper, just a down-hill runner.

    I am on that Mayo diet-starting today—one egg and orange juice and black coffee. I must get thin for Easter and not let you birds beat me in slenderness. It is hard work. I must stop writing and cook an egg.

Love, Ruby

Moses: Grandma Moses was an American octogenerian who became famous for her primitive paintings of rural scenes.

Earl Baily: Of Lunenberg, Nova Scotia, who had infantile paralysis when a child and later painted water colours with a brush held between his teeth.

Mar. 10/58

Dear Kay

Thanks for Sally's birthday money which she put in the bank with baby-sitting money and the four dollars she earned on Saturday at Mussers. That isn't very much pay for a long day, is it? She wants to be a lady of leasure this summer and play golf — she isn't interested in getting a job. Gosh you'd think we were millionairs or the next thing to it, eh? She doesn't realize how much it will cost to send her to university, thinks we just have to send her there as if she were going to high school. Life is not so easy as that around here. Fred finds business grim with all the people out of work — there are over 20,000 — no 2000 out of work here in Barrie (that is the trouble of having the radio on at the time I'm writing to you — I have one ear listening and every once in awhile I type what they are saying) I haven't been typing much lately I should keep it up in case I have to work for my living and if we have to put the kids through university and pay for it all. I wouldn't care if Sally worked hard but she doesn't study like Judy — she goes out or did go out twice this week and is going out with Don Reid tonite and Saturday to the show and the ice carnival and Sunday she goes to church from 9.30 till noon and then she falls asleep or studies or some boy comes around or she goes for a walk with a kid and at nite she goes to bed around 11 or 11:30. She is a sorta teacher's pet — according to the things we gather and whether they give her the marks honestly or not we'll never know — she sure doesn't work hard for them. We didn't know we had such a brain in public school as she is now. Bill is working harder these nites — he wasn't too pleased with his marks and we weren't either. 66% isn't too good for a grade niner so he is working harder and if he really wants to go thro to be a doctor he has to have lots of money so he realizes that he will have to buckel down. What a money out-take that will be, and years of hard work. He realizes that — or does he?

There now — don't you feel typewritten letters are less personel — cold and sorta not me. I always feel as if it's a newspaper story. Do you feel chilled after reading this?

Love, Ruby

Dear Kay

Haven't any news — I mended that slip you bought me years ago — it won't wear out, nor will those pants or that other slip — they sure were a good buy. I have worn them and worn them — the milk man is here now and I haven't any tickets — just a minute —

Well. We've just had our lunch, lettuce, cellery, orange juice and a hardboiled egg and about two tablespoons of salmon that was hanging around from last nite's sangridges that I made for us and the girl next door who came over to cash a $5 check because she was going to Toronto to meet her husband who is bringing home a business car and she is to drive their little Morse Miner home. He is getting a new car from his firm that he works for, they sold their car which was no good — he is a terrible driver — fast and a brake-jammer. So he got this small car for her and he was going to use the new business car but she said no, he could use the small car and send in an expense account for the big one and that way they would save money. Their collie pup ran away and I am sorta glad — think of a big dog tied up all day and barking his head off in their yard all summer.

Sally's having her boy freind and another couple in tonite — Bill is shaperone. We're going to play bridge at the Allan's next door. Their Rolf is sick again — they had the doctor on Sat. but Sue said he didn't know what's wrong with the kid. I guess it isn't much, they fuss so about everything that isn't just so — the mother is over there all the time, Sue just can't kope with a thing and now that she has 2 kids she is helpless. Rolf goes to kindergarten this fall and she will most likely not let him go over the hill alone — he never goes outside to play alone — they go out and stand around and watch him — they had a fence put around their back yard to keep him in with swings etc. but they never put him in it by himself.

Now we've had supper, I'm really a cheat on my diet — I ate a slice of ham and had home-made mayonnaise on lettuce and 1 egg. Ate an apple this aft too — do you think I'll get thin on that? Ate a dry piece of toast too — now for black coffee.

Love, Ruby

Dear Mother

I think my typewriter seems rather pale, don't you? We were suppose to go to the farm for Uncle Willie's birthday surprise party but Fred's brother wrote and said they're not having it and would later invite us for dinner with Uncle Willie. He is 80 tomorrow and Fred says they are all making a fuss over him cause he has a lot of money and is a widower with no children. I want Fred to sent him a card. But will he or won't he?

Haven't any news. The male man is doing the apartments. I have my ironing to do — I just draw and draw all the time — just did a sketch out the window. The squirrel has found a branch in the maple tree that the sap comes out of and he has been drinking it but today an icycle's hanging from the spot.

Well, well — the male man just brought a letter from Myrtle saying they are having Uncle Willie's party after all. They are all taking food and want us to stay over nite — but not for me — no farm for me in winter even though they do have a bathroom indoors. It's cold and I want to come home.

I painted the medicine chest yesterday — the yellow isn't the same as the yellow on the wall but it isn't too bad, will get some new curtains cause the ones I have are yellow too and don't match either. The painting made my throat soar but I can't complain about it now — it is at nite in bed that I notice it most.

Hurray, hurray — She just phoned for me to go to work on Thurs, Fri. and Sat. They're having a sale. I must go when I get the chance — they'll get someone else if I don't and I do want to work — life is so much more fun when you're kept busy — I don't get flashes if I'm on the go — minute I lie down I get them. I sleep better nites when I keep going — we're going to the birthday party — all the relations are going. We're taking 2 pounds of chocolates to Uncle Willie.

I'm watching a dance show on TV right now and I'm afraid this letter is full of mistakes because I can't do two things at the same time. Now I must quit.

I'll keep sending you my art — look at it from a distance.

Love, Ruby

Dear Mum

We had a wonderful time at the party for Uncle Willie — met all Fred's relations. Uncle Willie is a nice little old duck — recently sold his farm and thoroubred cattle for 80 thousand dollars.

Sally is cheering at a hockey game tonite. She still talks on the phone for an hour but in half-hour spells. Keep on sending those clippings of good advice to teenagers, she reads them and they might sink in. Right now she's talking to her latest — Don Reid — he gave her his ring — such fun — she's going steady. He's much nicer then Murry, he was nice too but so young. Don plays the piano and trumpet and is keen on good music — she finds him more interesting and more of a challenge. Murry was just fun and giggles. Don is in grade 12 and got 79% on his last report. He's an only child and a Brain. He takes organ lessons, plays the piano at school affairs and solo parts on the trumpet — I don't know how he ever got going with Sally — she's so tuneless. She's learning much from him in the composer line and an appreciation of music. He wants me to write words and he'll write the music. I'm trying hard to think about words but nothing comes into my head.

It's snowing. We're having sauerkraut for dinner — I'm hungry. We bought 3-1/2 dozen eggs at the farm — I should diet with them but I want to eat saurkraut tonite — oh me, that pork smells good — I'm starving.

No robins or crows yet — have you seen any? I bought Sally a breton sailor and me a garter belt on Sat. I'd like something new to square dance in — I've only my sack dress and Fred hates it and Jan's that I wore to church yesterday — they call it my grandmother dress — does she want it back?

Sally wants me to type a letter for her but I'm not going to do it. She was on the phone for half an hour and could have done it over and over again herself.

Bill bought himself some new ski boots for $30, regular 39.95 — a lot — but skiing is his favorite pastime — he's crazy about it and it's his own money that he earned. Here he is now and he's starved too.

Love Ruby

Breton sailor: A stiff, straight, wide brimmed hat with a flat crown and streamers down the back.

Dear Jan

I've a cold — one of those where my head is stupid yet my nose doesn't run and I feel stuffed inside sorta sore throaty etc, down deep in my chest. I went to bed with heating pad but it didn't loosen up. I'm going to work this aft if I'm called — I feel better when I'm up. Sally's fashion show is tonite, Kath and I are going to it. I'd really like to go to bed instead. Don't worry, I'm not sick, I just don't want to do anything. I just don't know what I want — not well, not sick — just — oh you know how you feel when a cold hits you and doesn't come out.

Haven't a thing to write about — I must get at my braiding. Bill is sad cause skiing may be over for this year — it was very wet yesterday. We don't know about coming home for Easter — Bill has let the Hade kids do his papers so much this winter that he isn't making much money and I hate to miss out at the store. There are so many wanting work there and I just need to ask off and She will get someone in my place but I want to work cause I like getting the money even though it isn't much but it helps and I want to help and too I will need to work if the kids want to go to college — and they both want to go so it will be important that I have a job and keep it. I still think I should have taken that full time one that was offered me but Fred said it would make me nervice to type and I wouldn't sleep nites — but opertunity only nocks once.

Oh kid, guess what — I nearly forgot — one of these days you'll be getting a carton weighing twenty-five pounds and full of chocolate covered raisins — you can send me the money any time. You see it was this way — I know how you birds love them and can't get them and when they got some in the store I bought five pounds and gave mother some and we ate the rest and I told the man in charge of the candy that next time he ordered some I'd buy more and he said he wouldn't re-order unless I'd take a whole box — well I thought a box meant maybe 10 lbs and you'd easily divide that between you and also maybe they wouldn't come in for a month or two — but they came in right away almost and a box has twenty-five pounds and what could I do but take it and send it home with the next person driving your way. Isn't it wonderful? Think — twenty-five pounds — only a little over 8 pounds apiece for each of you. That's not much really is it? I'll bet you'll eat them all in a week.

Love
Ruby

March 23/58

Dear Jan

Four of us went to the I.D.A. drug store and had a banana split, they always have them on at a special two for 29 at Easter time. I only ate one.

No wonder I am fat, Now I am waiting for a steak dinner. We buy those frozen minute steaks for 31¢, you get two in a package, real thin and good, though Fred thinks they are only 3 layers of pressed hamburg but they are done in 3 minutes and are truly good eating and we get them rather often — but tonite we are having the really true steak that is an inch thick. Happy day.

This is the reason why we didn't come home for Easter. The weather was so terrible and Fred had to go to the Brothers at 8.30 and to church after. We all went to church and Fred went back after taking us home to count the collection and I did the washing while he was away and then he took Sally for a driving lesson and Chester came down and we drew and then Fred and Sally came home and we went and ate ice cream and tonite Fred goes to church to put the money in the safe and we go to Chester's after to play bridge.

Tues. Sally goes by train with 3 other girls to Toronto on the same train as 15 boys who go up to a convention and are taking Sally and Beth. Beth has a grandmother the girls can stay with. They are going to a formal dance at Cassaloma. The boys are staying in Woodbine district and the grandmother lives more then 10 miles from there, how the boys will ever get the girls for the party is a mystery to me. It will cost a fortune for a taxi — busses and subway would take hours. Well I won't worry, but wouldn't it be awful to live in a big city where kids have to meet away from home because it's too far or too expensive to get there?

No more to write about, I am so hot at the moment that I must go outside to cool off. My glasses are steamed up from the heat of me — boy-oh-boy, I must be 100 degrees in the shade at the moment.

Love
Ruby

Mar. 29/58

Dear Jan

I love to write on lines on a clean sheet of paper, don't you? I didn't go to work because of a cold. I'm in bed, Fred's in Toronto, Sally stayed home from school this morning to help me. She went down street with Dad to get Bill some pants, his are so short — he needs a new jacket too — Sally wants to wear his old one as a blazer, she needs a new one badly and Bill's fits her perfectly. If only he had a new one for tomorrow nite — the ski dinner at the country club and his jacket is so small for him.

There now. I've just ordered a jacket for Bill from Eaton's. I hope it's his size and that I didn't make a mistake by not buying the cheaper one. He outgrows thing before they're worn out, but he'll be needing nicer things now that he's getting older and wearing jackets more. Yet I hope he does outgrow this — I want him as tall as Harry and I keep praying that he grows and grows, so I don't mind spending extra money on him for clothes, cause I do want him tall.

I can't get thin. I'm so fat, people tell me "Oh you're fatter," Darn, I can't eat NOTHING. I'm always hungry and I keep saying I won't eat but I eat twice as much. And guess what — I found candies I'd bought at Xmas time up in the attic hole on Sunday. Those carmels in colored paper and those thin butterscotch wafer types. What a find! I ate carmels all day Sunday and now they are gone but I still have the butterscotch wafers — wish they were pepermint with chocolate.

No news — I bought a new blouse — sleeveless with a wee collar, 97¢. Sally took it over and wore it on Sat. nite. I don't mind, I like sleeves for my fat arms. I must not eat, I must not eat, I should write that out a 100 times like school kids as punishment, then maybe I'd stick to it.

Must stop now — such a no-good letter — only cold and blouse talk. I got up and ate cheese and crackers and spagetti — I was hungry — then I made some lemon marmalade with a bitter taste — I love the peel. I feel better up then in bed. I'd love to go to the show tonite but someone from the store might see me and I'd lose my job.

A dog came here this aft — don't know who he belongs to. I fed him 6 or 8 slices of bread — he was so hungry, poor dog.

Love, Ruby

Dear Jan

I'm up out of bed, hope I don't get worse — I sure feel good at the moment. Had a bath and washed my hair — couldn't stand it any longer — dried it by the fire, making me a cup of tea now. Wish you were here to drink some with me. Kids wanted me to stay in bed — they did the breakfast dishes — gee are they good, wonder what's up? Now isn't that mean? But they don't help very often.

Sue has her baby out, she's wheeling it slowly up and down the street while her mother is looking after Rolf who is pushing a monkey in his gocart. Whee my tea's hot — really Sue's mother is here all the time — I think Sue is embarrassed yet what would she do without her — she's so helpless.

What a gorgeous looking day from inside — it must be wonderful out — springlike — up to 50. I wish I could go out. Starlings are going into birdhouse — I hope the squirrel chases them. Oh there he is now — I was just going to say he hasn't been here for ages — 2 starlings are sitting on a limb in front of his house but he seems to ignore them. Kid next door to Sue — Linda is outside — poor kid — noone to play with on this side of the street except Rolf and they won't let him play; they make him go for walks with them or stay indoors. There are 5 kids all Linda's size across the road in the apartments and they're having such fun and they're so cute (from here) and Linda just stands and looks at them — how she'd love to go over and play with them, I'll bet.

Now I'm trying to write words for Don Reid to compose music to. Oh to hit a jackpot. I wonder what to write about — love — passed love — oh I must get going and write — I've only been dreaming. Have another cup of tea? I ask myself. Sure. My sweet potato is growing, has roots and 2 sprouts, I am anxious to see what the thing will look like, haven't seen one growing for years.

We are going to hear Guy Lombardo when he comes on the 14th of April for my birthday present. Wonderful eh?

Love, Ruby

Guy Lombardo: A successful New York based jazz band leader who grew up in London, Ontario.

Hi mum

No one wrote me last week, have you been sick? I'm still home from work. When I go to the unemployment to collect they give me $9. When I work 3 days at the store I get $11 there and $1 from the unemployment — the only thing is I get stamps to show that I worked and they go towards unemployment insurance next year. But I don't use up all my unemployment money each time anyway so there's no sence working when I'm not feeling well. My cold doesn't want to break up — it sure is down deep inside me. I cough if I talk too much. She called this morning for me to go in but I had washed and hung out my clothes and had to go to get maple syrup — I'm fussy about getting first run — it is so good though Fred thinks it is too mild and not so maple a flavour but I think it tastes like the stuff you use to get when we were kids — I got 5 full quarts from one gallon and we have eaten one jar already.

Bill had his last skiing on Sunday — he said you could just see the snow melt out there on the hill — one minute you could jump over the mud to snow — the next minute you couldn't because the snow would be gone. He left my thermos out in a snow pile so we had to drive out to get it last nite. I hated not to when the thing cost $1.98 yet the gas out would cost nearly a $1 but we hadn't been out all day cept to church and we had eaten a turkey dinner that Fred got so the kids could make sangridges for school lunches — sure is easy to get meals with it around.

I wore my suit to church and my last year's black hat — Sally got the new hat of the family this year — a darling white straw sailor with white velvet ribbon down the back and a little pink rose. Too young for me.

I voted on my way with the syrup, the chap at Fred's office is running for liberal but no one thinks he will get in cause his opponent has been in for years and years, he is too old but this is a conservitive town and Fred says the fellow from his office is just a stuge for the liberals until the conservitive dies. It would be fun to see him get in though, he has four kids and a real skinny wife. He sure would get a surprise if he won.

Kath's clothes line broke this morning and down fell all her clean wash in the mud. I must bring mine in now.

Love, Ruby

April 2/58

Dear Mother

Maybe now that you've fallen again and hurt your knee we had better not come for the week-end. We can come another time — I'd hate to bring my cold along. With Jan's cold and Tommy's and mine and your leg you'd be better off without us buzzing around. With us there you wouldn't stay off your foot and I know you must.

I don't blame Kay for wanting to go to Europe again, I sure would if I were in her shoes. I'm not sure but I think I want to see Canada first. I haven't been west and I've always wanted to see Alaska — why, I don't know but I've always had a yen to see the flowers grow so fast, and the midnight sun. I don't suppose I'll ever get either places but it is fun thinking about it and having a bit of money in the bank to make you feel you could go if you really wanted to. With my paid-up insurance policy I have almost $2000 so I could take a trip if I really got going. I keep thinking I must work while I still can — when I'm older I can go — if my health is as good as your's has been. By the time I'm 60 or 65 they'll fire me at the store so I might as well work till I can't — if it isn't too late. But I sure would like to see Canada first — I'd hate to go to Europe and say I hadn't crossed Canada. Fred has crossed so he wouldn't care, he'd like to take the kids east — I would rather go west or any place where I haven't been.

Haven't any news. Bill's out playing golf with 3 boys and their lunch, it's muddy but he wears rubber boots. He's in a concert on Fri. nite at the Memorial Centre, he has a solo part of 4 notes with his french horn in one piece and wants me to go to hear him. Sally has a mother and daughter coffee party on the 30th and I'm ask to a shower the same nite — I wonder if I can go to both at the extreme ends of town — if only I could drive I'd make Dad stay home that nite and take the car.

Looks like rain — rain or snow — but I don't mind as long as it isn't windy, I hate wind. I use to like it when I was young but I guess it's you coming out in me — you always hated it too, didn't you? Must be off — Sally's boy friend sent me a 25¢ Easter card — guess he likes me, eh?

Love Ruby

P.S. The liberal chap in Fred's office didn't get in. Conservatives always win here.

Dear Kay

Thanks a million for the darling blouse. I just love it. So does Sally but I have to get a smaller size. I'm really a 14. I tried it on and it droops off my shoulders on both sides. Sally is taking it to Simpsons at noon. She passes there twice a day. Thanks so much, it's just what I needed too. It's the sweetest blouse I've ever seen and I've never owned such an expensive one cept the one you gave me from Key West. I'm afraid that's seen it's day, wearing out under the arm, I've mended it but I think this year is its last. I'm going to take the pattern off it when it's of no use. Thanks again for my honey of a blouse, I sure love it.

April 24 — my birthday and George Miller's — Shirley Harmer's husband — I always liked George on TV. I should send him a card. I know 2 girls and a grandmother who have birthdays on my birthday too. One year I had 27 daffodils in bloom on my birthday today I've only 4 in tight buds. I'd like to bring them home to mother.

I transplanted my tomatoes I started growing from those Maytime affairs you buy at Woolworth's, add water and in a couple of days they're growing. I think I'll have a bath, pick me some rhubarb from the garden and cook it — it's just up a bit, but enough for one dish. My parsley's growing too.

I bought material to make Sally a dress — skirt and top. I wish she'd sew it herself — she'll never learn to make clothes if she doesn't try. Here's a sample of cloth, it will cost $3.11. She'd like me to make all her clothes so she wouldn't look like everyone else but it's too much for me when I'm working — I'm not good at it and I get flashes though I might be better if I kept at it and it's cheaper then buying things, that's for sure, but Time, Time, Time — where is it?

We went to closing square dancing on Fri. nite, boy I sure get tired after and never get to sleep till 3.30. I'm really beat — I look tired too, dark circles under my eyes and I think my hair needs cutting, it's so long and thick and heavy, I hate it. Wish housecleaning and Sally's dress were done. Always something.

Love, Ruby

George Miller and Shirley Harmer: A husband-and-wife team of singers who were often heard on CBC radio programmes.

Dear Mum

Just finished washing and I've a wet foot from pouring out the wash water. What was I going to send to you for Kay? Was I dreaming or what? Seems there was something I said I'd send in an envelope to you for her — but what? I can't remember. Do you? Guess she is in Portugal by now, wasn't it there that she was going to land? Wouldn't landing in Lisbon be wonderful?

We went to see the terrible fire down town then we had a lovely salad supper with cold meat and frozen strawberries for desert.

Sally had a nose-bleed — she's overtired. Got another badge, a crest, at school. She's gotten one every year so far. Next year she hopes to get the highest award — the gold felt B for Barrie. She's going to try hard, she has to have 10 points — got 7 this year though she only needed 5 or 6. Her boy friend is having his 17th birthday today — he's a nice kid and very well liked by all the kids and the teachers especially. Comes from a nice family but don't worry, Sally isn't marrying him — one doesn't stay with one beau forever — least I didn't. I doubt if she'll settle down to marriage at her age — both want to go to college. She's not thinking in terms of marriage — and sex is far from her mind. She's just having fun and I don't worry about her at all. She's always saying to Billy, it's your life and if you ruin it it's your fault. She's really a great thinker, the teachers say, doesn't study so hard that she's the top pupil but one that's got a brain and uses it. We're proud of her and wish Bill would be more like her. Though he's working harder. He's still not thinking as an adult — still plays with kids. Oh well he's only 14 — 2 years makes a difference.

Minister on radio just said people without children should read Psalm 37. I wonder why? I must look that up.

John and his friends had a golf tournament — 50¢ fee with 9 entered. He had fun but lost the cup he won last time. I have a touch of disentry.

Love Ruby

May 10/58

Dear Jan

You should see my gorgeous lovely little new grey lamb jacket!!!!!!!!!!!!! Am I ever thrilled to think that I earned enough and saved enough to go into a store and buy one for myself—just like that without haveing to ask anyone if I could or having to wait forever till Fred could give me enough money to pay for it. And it's such a darling, I love it. I hope you come down soon to see it. I haven't worn it yet—it's too warm out—worse luck. It has slits at the sides like a man's shirt—is the length of a station wagon coat but shorter, back is slightly full but not really—just a nice hanging fullness. It's really a beauty. Oh kid, and it's mine. I bought it.

Raining, raining, raining, And Bill wants to go fishing. My tomatoes are up, my foursithia is growing, Fred bought a load of top soil for the garden and I wish he'd get another cause if the guy behind ever puts shrubs across the borderline we'll be closed in for good and we'd have to wheelbarrel it up to the garden from the front and it would be horrid to do. But I can't talk him into it. I'd like to have a garden that would really grow, last year ours was a flop.

There are tiny leaves on our trees now—yesterday they were only in buds. This is a good rain. Back yard is so pretty when apple blossoms are out, our pear tree has some blossoms out now but it's only got one branch.

Bill gave me a box of chocolates for Mother's Day. We ate them after church. He always talks about you eating the 5 or 2 pound box all at once—says he should buy you one when we go up there so he can help you eat them—I only let him eat the top layer of mine, I'm saving the rest. Now I'll have to be careful, mayn't get too fat for my dear little jacket—although it has lots of room round the bottom if I should spread out more—but then it wouldn't look nice and I want to be proud of it and give it the best setting I can.

Come down soon and look at my prize and my joy—my darling fur jacket.

Love
Ruby

Dear Mum

We're out in front watching the cars go by the house. I'm going with Fred to see what's the hold-up. Cars are lined up passed our place all the way from that stop light eight blocks away. Traffic is terriffic. I went out on the street and told people how to get out of it by turning up Brookdale — it was fun but my kids were horrified at me doing it. It's the only way to get traffic moving — a cop should direct it. The line-up is terrible — boats on top of cars and all. Bill wants me to stop helping — cars are thinning out now — no, I guess it was just a green light farther down. Fred's gone to Chester's now for a beer. I'm so glad I'm here in my front yard and not in a car on the road — such a mess — bumper to bumper. Now the bottle-neck must be just about over. A black cat just passed in a car. I must get supper, everyone's hungry.

Now we've eaten — traffic's over too — no tie-up now. Just cars going by as usual. Kids are going golfing and I'm going to do dishes while Dad drives them out. Bill came 2nd in golf tournament this morning, he got a belt worth $1.50 — his fee was $1, his caddy got 40¢ so he's up 10¢ but he does have the prize though not the cup.

Sue Allan didn't talk to me for three days because I was cross at her kid Rolf for pulling up my tulips — but wouldn't you be? Her husband's on great terms with me though and sure didn't want Sue to be cross and now she's really friendly and chatty again. All is well, the kid is their's to worry over, not mine. Thank goodness.

Fred and I are drinking coffee now, wish you were here. I mopped up the house then I slept — it's turned cold and windy — it sure is blowing. Sally has a chance to work at a lodge for $35 a week this summer but I'm not sure it's a good idea, are you? She's only 16 and she really is pretty — at least we think so — and you never know what kind of men might stay at those places and try to enviggle the girls into their room or whatever. She's so innocent that I don't want her getting into anything nasty that might spoil her way of looking at life. There's plenty of time for that kind of learning when she's much older. But she can't sit around here doing nothing all summer or playing golf.

Love
Ruby

May 16/58

Dear mum

How's life? Thro housecleaning? I didn't do any today, but I'll have it done by the 24th if you come down and if I don't get lazy.

Here's a card from Kay in Ireland, I was cross at Fred, he gave away the stamps off it to the Hade kids. I didn't even see them. What are Irish stamps like? Do they have a harp or shamrocks or potatos or what? I have a small stamp collection that I've had since a child — made me so mad having him give them away.

Sally went to a dance at the Y last nite with her Don. He went to Toronto on Thur and brought her a locket — a gold chain with a square gold mirrorlike affair with engraved flowers and plain gold on the other side that you can see yourself in. She was thrilled. I heard her say she's going to stay in Fri. nite and study, exams will soon be here.

It rained yesterday. I have 2 daffodils out, I'm going to dig up the flower bed by the hedge and have it in grass, it's a mess now with nothing but iris and peanies and bleeding hearts in it — too hard to keep up with me working and Fred won't be bothered.

This is Mac and Myrtle's annerversary, but they won't be celebrating it — least not a party or anything that envolves us. Can't seem to spell annerversary today.

Fred went up north from Tues to Fri. with another agent and did fairly well. The other chap lives in Orilia and Fred wanted to help him. I got some beautiful geranium slips at the golf club last nite — they have hundreds and in 5 different colors. Bill played golf and Fred and I went to church and Sally had homework to do and her ex boy-friend came up to see her in the aft. I should take a laxative.

I bought home baking from a church group yesterday — cherry pie — date bread and different kinds of squares and tarts — they were super, the pie's gone — not too hot, but not bad, cocoanut squares were favorites, date cookies got soft, bread wasn't too good — one can't tell about baking like that. Well — a feast then a famon. Tonite we're having stew out of a can.

Love, Ruby

Dear Jan

There was something special I had to say to you, now I've forgotten what it was — will probably think of it later. Fred's taking tickets down at the Fair grounds and he gets paid $5.25 for it. Hell drivers or something, wild car racing. I hope he comes home ok, I hate those hell driver shows — always afraid they'll run into people, I made Fred promise to go high up on the seats of the bleachers if he stayed to watch them.

My hair is a mess — Sally says let it grow long. I bought 5 records on Sat. 29¢ apiece — the Nutcracker suite, Chopin and Schubert, Skater's Waltz, Libestraum piano pieces and e flat such and such — I love them and when they wear out we'll throw them out cause they're not expensive. Our $4.50 record we've played so much it has a thump in it but we sure enjoyed it — Matavani in the Imortal Classics. Did we ever love it — turned it on every nite throughout the winter and went to sleep by it — one side of the record plays for 2 minutes — and the nice part is we don't have to get out of bed to turn off the machine, it goes off itself.

Bill's ski pal's father died suddenly — 44 years old. We knew him and took Bill to see him — his 1st dead person. He didn't want to go but I made him and Johnnie was glad and phoned Bill last nite to collect homework for today. He's a nice kid. Bill was afraid to go cause he didn't know what to say.

Still don't know what I wanted to tell you. I emptied the bottom drawer of the chest of drawers in our bedroom and put a box of flakes and mothballs in it and laid my fur jacket flat in — fits perfectly and it's ok there I guess till about Sept. they say they haul them out of storage then. I can hardly wait to wear it — must watch for skirts on sale to go with it.

Haven't any news — still don't know what I wanted to tell you, must start ironing now. Ches and Mabel want to sell their house and buy a dish washer — she has exzima and has to keep her hands out of water. Still can't think what I wanted to write about. Did you ask me a question in your last letter?

Love, Ruby

Dear Mum

I've my washing pumping so I'm hurrying with this — we went over
to Chester last nite, Mabel was away for the weekend and not coming
home till today but arrived last nite at 9.30 all worn out because she
hich-hicked. Her car broke down 10 miles out of town and she was all
alone. Fred and Ches drove out to get her luggage and to see if they could
start the car — the battery was dead. They pushed it for 2 miles then got
the motor league to get it. We got home just after the news, leaving
Mabel and Chester shouting at each other.

I finished my book on the duchess of Winsor — she's quite a
gal — and what an interesting book — she sure was out to catch the
Prince of Wales, I'd say. I like her less then I did and don't feel sorry for
either of them since I read it. She doesn't say so but she's just a social
climber, out to get everything. Now I guess they sit thinking of their
past, they'd never dare to bust up.

Haven't any news — Isabel said Sue's Rolf nearly hit her on the
head with a shovel the other day, the big digging shovel — missed her by
an inch. She was shaking and all upset for days — said he nearly killed
her. She said if they don't train that kid, she will and he won't come on
their property unless he does what they tell him to. He's really a beggar
but it's not his fault, his parents didn't teach him right from wrong. He
cut his finger on a knife he found over at Mabel's and went home
crying — his dad came over and asked Mabel if the knife was open and
she said no, they're never open — 2 wee souvenir pen-knives an inch long
that she has on a chain in the door with her door-key. Mabel was on the
phone when Rolf was there and he took them and opened one, cut his
finger and went home screaming. They took him to the doctor for a shot
and later went over to Mabel's again to see if the knife was open — didn't
believe Rolf had opened the knife himself — they never believe their
Rolfie can do anything himself. Mabel said she felt they thought she
opened the blade for Rolf to cut himself on purpose, said it took Rolf's
grandmother all her strength to speak to her after blaming her. They've
had other trouble with Rolf too and chase him home now when he
comes — so you see I'm not the only one in the neighbourhood.

Love Ruby

Dear Jan

It's quarter to nine and I have to go to work, kids have left and Fred's still in the bathroom. I'm glad I have a chance to work the odd morning — it helps with the money. I bought a dress for Sally on Sat. Now she's not sure she likes it — saw a girl with one like it at school and wanted me to take it back. I said no, you take it back, then she said, oh I guess it's all right. Fred said on Sat. nite she didn't like it — he seemed to sense it — yet in the store she was gloomy cause I didn't fall all over it like she did. These kids!!!!!

A girl asked Bill to a weiner roast on Sat. his first real date. The mother of the girl drove her home and Bill walked home. She's a nice girl, Sally said. Bill was happy — I'm glad he doesn't run after girls.

Now Fred's eating breakfast — I've bed made and dishes washed. Haven't any news. I've so much to do — housecleaning, garden to put in, clothes to mend, head to wash. Should I plant a hedge up there on the stone wall or plant flowers? Hedge would grow tall and shade the garden so I guess a border of all my different flowers, eh? They're all perenials and no trouble to look after — peanies, bleeding hart, iris, solomon seal, lemon lilies, flocks, fouroclocks and another tall yellow plant, monx flour and a blue one I don't know the name of and a red one and one more feathery blue one. I guess that's all the different kinds I have cept a rose colored colombine and hollyhocks. And shrubs — hydrange, lilac, pink honeysuckle, orange blossom, barbary, bridle reath and a white shrub that has a flower like a Persian lilac in August.

We're having the piano tuned — must clean it before the man comes. It hasn't been tuned since we bought it and will cost 10 or 12 dollars or more so I'm glad to work this morning to get out of the racket of it. The big cheese is here from head office today and I was called in to clean up the jewellery bins. Must put on my lipstick now and get going.

Love, Ruby

June 4/58

Dear Mum

I bought a chemise — I love it. The colour is so flattering and young-looking on me — a beautiful deepish rose color — Mrs. Cash at the store sold it to me and said That sure is your color — it is very becoming and makes you look like a girl. I'm saving it for good for awhile. I'll wear it to church with my new black assessories.

Today I worked at such and such: first — I mended 3 blouses and my leopard dressing gown that had seems ripped, then I got breakfast, put kids bicycles out of garage and made sangridges for them and off they went. Breakfasted with Fred and we put in the garden. I sprinkled after and washed down the house outside and mopped up inside and shook out mats, ironed and fixed my new chemise — oh I love it on me — then I ironed Sally's dress, sprinkled the garden, got meals and did dishes and beds and sewed, read my book and a magazine. Now I must do dishes again. We've more baby robins — robins always have 2 batches, you should have left your nest there, Mabel said, not sure if she's right — our robin built in an old crow's nest on our front veranda evetrough.

No news — we had pork chops for dinner. I'm trying to reduce — sure takes will power. Went to Roger's last nite to show them my chemise and they liked it, said it's not too chemisie — Fred's not too keen on it but he's getting to like it better as he hears others admire it — all there is to it is 3 buttons and belt over hips but it sure is pretty. $5.50 on sale — with my 20% off, regular 19.98 I'd never have bought a chemise if it hadn't been so cheap and so lovely.

Now I'll get on Sally's bike and mail this. And when I get home I'll finish Sally's dress that I've been making for ages. Fred won a cigarette lighter at the office.

Oh mum, I love my chemise — I feel so fashionable — I wish you could see it — why don't you come down?

Love, Ruby

Dear Mum

I bought a red hat to go with my black suit and a red scarf, they'll look nice with my fur jacket. I'll save them for fall or next spring — like I did with my black straw — it's much like it — small and guess the price — 87¢ regular $3.98. Just what I needed. The scarf and hat match — they're perfect and I love them. Still not sure what to wear with my rose chemise — I wore it to work to show it off and everyone liked it on me — I'm saving it for goodish — yet I must get my wear out of it — the color's so nice on me.

Bill's still doing papers — it's 6.30 and the rest of us have eaten a fish dinner — was it ever good — oh I love fish. Got a card from Kay today, she sent me one with a cat — he's so darling, I keep him hanging in the livingroom — I just can't part with him yet to show you — he's so cute — even has dirt in his ears.

I'll iron tonite — Fred has to see 3 men. It's so cold outside I have my tomato plants inside. Kay will soon be home from Europe — time flies. Sally baby-sat across the road last nite, she's through school all but exams now. Mary Mandell was in the store yesterday wearing her daughter's suit, she looked stunning — painted eye shadow on her eyes. She says she's fat, wants to diet — what I wouldn't give to get into Sally's clothes — and she says she wants to diet.

Bill isn't home yet — can't figure it out he's on his bicycle. Tonite we'll watch TV. I'm going to buy a new white purse, I think.

Here's Bill now, I'll get his supper. I'm lazy, my coffee's too hot. I guess I'd better sign off — Bill wants to tell me his news — nothing much.

Before I forget — Mother what's wrong with you. Sure you can play bridge — what makes you think you can't? Did you get a booby prize?

Maybe you worked too hard. Come down here and play with us.

Love, Ruby

June 14/58

Dear Kay

A quicky before I get dressed for work. I washed — it's so windy it makes me sick — Hope the summer's not all like this, if so I'm not going on holidays. I hate the wind. Fred took off storms on Sat. and I wish they were still on, it's so drafty.

Haven't any news. We have moles in our stone wall and a mouse in our cellar and baby squirrels in our birdhouse — they go in and out. I've a sore throat and a pain below my chest — it may be imagination but I sure have been worrying about it. I've not lost weight over it unfortunately but I'd best go to doctor and let him do the worrying. My throat is sore and the pains are there, I know they are — yet I forget all about them when I'm on a picnic or working. I'm so fat. I must reduce today. Had strawberry short-cake for breakfast left over from yesterday — and was it ever good!

Wind's getting worse — I'll go nuts if it keeps up — you should see the dust fly — I'm going out after my wash — it's terrible.

There. Got my wash in. The Agent's convention is on — wish we were at it, I've never been to one. Makes me mad that Fred doesn't sell more to qualify but no sense in getting that way. He just never seems to make it — for 14 years I've been waiting and hoping to go. He's getting his first made-to-fit suit — there's a sale on and he really needs one. Bill got 2 pair of pants — his were too tight across the front and looked awful though that's the style for young boys. Got him a suede jacket for 9.99 and a new shirt and shorts and a bathing suit and a hat for Dad — that's all I'm getting them and Sally her new dress and the one I made her and my adorable chemise — that's all I'm spending from now on — my money just melts.

I hope our garden is better then last year — we didn't get anything worth while out of it with Rolf next door picking our tomatoes. They keep him in his back yard now — fenced up — and Sue plays with him there. A good place for him. Here's her mother coming again. She comes every day to look after Sue and her kids — people behind us thought she lived with Sue — she does too — only sleeps at home.

Must stop now — go easy — life wasn't built in a day — but this wind sure could nock it down in one.

Love, Ruby

P.S. Went to doctor — nothing wrong.

June 16/58

Dear Jan

Chester and Mabel bought a coral color Chev and a dishwasher, we're going up to their house to see them. Our piano is in good shape now, the chap thought we should get $100 or 150 for it if we put an ad in the paper in Aug. or early Sept. when kids start taking lessons. He says it's a good one, but Bill hates to see us get rid of it, he might want to take lessons again. Plays every once in a while.

Mary Hade came to see me yesterday aft — I had just baked a chocolate cake without a recipe — sorta followed one but not altogether — and was it ever a success — I was glad I had it to give her a piece — she likes my fur coat and chemise.

Baby squirrels are growing. Girl next door on the other side is still away. We had her husband in for a meal on Sun. He's a sunny little guy — nice but sorta show-off, nervice type, talks big for a little guy. Told Sally he went to Queens for 3 years but his english is terrible at times — I doubt if a university student even though he didn't graduate would speak so badly. Anyway we like him.

Does Judy want to come here while you're away this summer? We'd love to have her. Send her on the train and we'll meet her. Gee I hope she comes — we're all so excited — she could play duets with Sally's boy friend. Oh happy day — we'd love to have her stay till you come home. How about it? And we'll write to Tommy every day he's at camp so he'll get a letter every day and not get homesick and we could go up to the lake and get him if he is homesick and bring him here with Judy. He just needs to write us and we'll take off after him.

Gosh — poor Uncle David — poor guy — he's got no will power. Wish he'd live with us for awhile — we haven't any liquor but I'm afraid to have him here if he'd get bored he'd go out and buy it and I'm afraid of him drinking and getting the way he does. I'd never be able to handle him, that's for sure. What makes him drink — his conscience bothers him or what? He sure is a tearer. I hope he snaps out of it. But I doubt it — he's like me and my reducing — always tomorrow.

Love
Ruby

Dear Mum

A perfect day—and all for me. I ironed and washed yesterday and worked a 1/2 day at the store so today is for me. I'm getting paid as if I'm working because it's a holiday and I'm going to do nothing but make meals today—and not very special ones either. Bill's already had his lunch and is off to the golf course, Sally is sleeping and Fred's going to see a man.

On Sat. nite Ron Hade phoned from 30 miles away that his car broke down and he wanted Fred to pick him up, Mary and the kids were with him. I was in bed but got out and went with Fred. It was after 11 when Ron called and we got back at 3 in the morning. Fred went to church, I went to the back yard in shorts and got sun on my legs then took shortbreads to a woman from the store who had an operation.

The results came out yesterday—Sally—Eng. comp 61, lit 58—you see she doesn't read—hist. 87, math 74—she really got upset—teacher felt badly because she should have had over 90 in her best subject—she was off all through her exams—physic 90, french comp 80, authors 80, phys ed 73, geom 61—average 73%. Bill—Eng comp 68, lit 63—he doesn't read either—social studies 75, math 60, science 74, french 64, music 80, drafting 58, electric 69—average 67%.

We're disappointed that Sally didn't get 75% average—she was a reck the day she tried math, the teacher even stood beside her at exam and told her to take it easy she seemed so excited and upset that he noticed it and she knew it and flopped badly—only 74. Oh well both passed and I guess that's all to ask of them.

We want to come to Stratford sometime when the Shakespeare play Sally took at school is on. Do we get tickets now or when? We all want to go—good for kids to see something educational, eh? Especially English.

We're planning to go to Halifax the last 2 weeks in August, kids are looking forward to seeing the ocean, Sally will be able to help with the driving. She is driving herself to work every day with Fred sitting beside her. She drives home at noons too before traffic is too heavy. We don't think we'll tent. We'll stay at motels—only 2 or 3 nites on the road there and back—in Halifax we can stay at cousin Olive's and in Bridgewater at the Mortons and in Yarmouth at the Joneses.

Love, Ruby

Off: We called menstruation being "off the floor" or simply being "off." Mother wouldn't let us use the more common term "the curse."

Dear Kay

Welcome home — glad you had a wonderful trip, wish I'd been with you. I'm weary tonite — it's the wind and the sun, Bill played golf morn, noon and nite, Sally's making a short skirt for cheerleading the lacross team, and she hates sewing. My machine needs an overgoing — making rugs on it didn't help it any and noone oils it. Fred promised to clean it in varsole but hasn't as yet. Flo gave Sally a dress — it's a honey and Sally likes it. Flo is really tall and skinny and Sally is so tiny but the dress fits not too badly with the hem turned up.

I'm taking nerve medicine and I've broken out in an itchy rash on my knee, it's all red. Must stop taking it, it's happend with this medicine before. I went for a check-up two weeks ago and I'm ok but have nerves. I sorta worried about myself because I had a sore throat and it wouldn't stop. I think it's from the air conditioner in the store — I have to wear a sweater it's so cold and there are 3 cold air things just above our counter and Mrs. Grafton at the store had a bosom operation last week and scared everyone but she's ok so we're all well and happy again.

Haven't any news, glad you're home. Mother phoned tonite, if we had only known noone was meeting you we'd have come. I was just busting to see your plane land. I said to Fred how I'd love to meet Kay, wish we had now. Wish Uncle Dave would straighten up. Bill wonders if all the kids got together to write him if it would help. What a shame he can't stop drinking. He was so good there and phoned me and was so happy — then bingo. I don't know what one can do with him.

Well, kid, I'm glad you're safe. Come on down with mother. She wants to come. She seemed sad tonite — please come down eh? Our garden's growing. We ate lettuce today and radishes. I'm hungry for a soft boiled egg — will have one for lunch. We had waffles for breakfast, left over from a bed-time snake last nite. Sally saw a meteor on Monday nite.

Love, Ruby

Dear Mum

I'm in the back yard, it's lovely out here on the old picnic table. Man behind us is going to put up a fence — it's too dangerous driving his car in and out in winter, they're afraid they might slip into our garden. I'd like to get some manure in before they close us off. Gosh it's a lovely morning, are you sitting in your back yard? It's going to be 80 today, already too hot for me now in the sun, I'm not a sun tan feen any more, I don't care if I'm not tanned — I'm not wearing shorts any more. Sally and Fred say I'm too old so out they go — no use trying to look young, I'd rather stay dressed nice in dresses and they're just as cheap as good shorts and cooler.

Now I must tell you about Mavis — she wrote that they're moving to Toronto where Bing works, buying a small house there. Mavis's dad lives with them and it's not working too well having him with them so they want to put him in a nursing home and he's not keen on going. He was hurt in the first war and is lame and is finding it tough to walk more and more so Mavis feels she should put him somewhere where they've nurses to help him — less trouble all round. The dad is visiting all his children for 3 weeks then he'd be so glad to settle down again for the winter with Mavis but she doesn't want him and the others don't want him either. Tough when you get old and have something wrong with you. You go easy mother and rest and save your money — you never know how you'll need it. That's why we tell Sally and Bill to save. We don't want to spend all ours on them so that we won't have any when we're old cause they won't want us either.

Must stop now, Bill's up and wants a pair of pants pressed — he should have another pair then I'd not have to always wash out and iron a pair when the other is dirty. Our kids are at a stage when they do this and that — go here and there — they don't want to do anything but what they want to do. They're happy working to make money for themselves — and they're saving it — you don't have to worry about them.

Come down, eh? You never come. I often wonder if my neighbours think you and I don't get along together.

Love
Ruby

July 28/58

Dear Kay

Thanks for the coke cooler. We'll take care of it. Sure you don't need it? Isn't it exciting us owning a tent, air matresses and sleeping bags? Now we can sleep 12 here beautifully, the whole family with mother in our bed. Isn't it going to be wonderful? I'm so glad we got it. Gee — 4 extra beds. We have 5 double beds, 4 sleeping air mattresses, 3 single beds and one can sleep on the lazy-boy chair — that makes 14 really. Gosh — 14 people can sleep in our little house. Isn't that lovely? We hope you'll come soon.

Haven't any news. I'm so full of chocolate coated raisins. They have them at the store and I bet I ate 1/2 a pound of them today. Each time I went near them at the candy counter I helped myself to a handful. I'm sick of them now, I couldn't look one in the face.

We still have to get the 4 mattresses and 3 bags and a Coleman stove — I hope we haven't forgotten anything important to take on our trip and that the weather will be nice and not too cold nites. Sally has to get a license so she can do some of the driving. I hope she doesn't make me nervice.

Bill is playing the piano again, now that Sally's boy friend is so musical and plays the organ for weddings. He's a nice kid. You should come down and meet him.

Our apple trees are loaded this year but Fred didn't spray them. Wish our pear tree was as big, they're all the same age — 10 years — but the pear had its branches broken off by the kids, we've a stake and a string round it now to train it. When it's big it will hide us from the neighbour's and we won't have to close the bathroom window blind any more. Happy day — such a nuisance.

My coffee pot is empty now — so I'll get moving. Kid at store has 24 hour measles — ever heard of them? No, I hadn't either. Don't ever wash an orlon sweater and put it in the sun — it turns yellow — Sally did it with her new banlon and it's really a reck. Bye now, come down soon, Thanks again.

Love, Ruby

Dear Kay *

Thanks for the nice week-end and the meals. Many thanks. And for letting us spend all our time raving about our wonderful trip to the Maritimes and Quebec. We'll have to settle down now for the winter months. I guess we've had our last trip before Christmas. How about you all coming down here? Thanksgiving perhaps, eh? Dave promised you'd come. Bring the whole gang. Remember we can sleep 14 people now. Isn't that lovely? Please come for sure and come soon.

Fred's having breakfast now so I must rush — RUSH — say I just wrote that word when Fred knocked a full milk bottle off the table onto the floor and did it ever break in a thousand pieces — just slivers. I've just got it cleaned up now and Fred's off to work.

I just finished washing my hair last nite — not even combed — when Alex Moskel came over for a box and Chester came too. Alex was interested in our trip — they were here the night we were leaving. They go down south at Easter and tent by boat but never by car. Has never been east so wanted to hear all about it. It's wonderful telling. One of the best parts of a trip, isn't it?

Well we're off in a run again. Kids off to school each morning at 8.30 with their lunches — what a job making sandwiches etc. I get sick of making them — Sally made them last nite.

I must go to the library — they have a record bar and I must get German records to see if I can learn anything. Must do some sketching too, I was thinking of going to art class but maybe I'll think about that later. I must get my rug connected — stuff's braided and will be eaten by moths if I don't soon start sewing it together. Oh kid there's so much to do if only I'd get going — I must get a heavy skirt to wear with my darling fur jacket — I'm busting to wear it but it's not quite time yet, is it? I must think about a hat for it and Sally needs a new coat for good. I'd like a camel hair for her — they say they wear well — or else a Harris tweed. I must get going. Come down soon, thanks again.

Love, Ruby

Dear Jan

Today we're going to the Moskel's cottage — for supper — the invite came as a shock — we didn't know we were such pals of theirs though they've asked us to pitch our tent at their cottage before but we haven't. They're out Beaverton way on a lake I never heard of — hope we find it ok. Sally's not going — has a date. Oh the phone —

Long distance. Mrs. Moskel doesn't want us today. She'd rather it was a nicer day to have us at the cottage — it's small, she says, and all would have to be inside and it's nicer outdoors at a place like that so we'll go again — she said —

The janitor of the collegiate dropped dead in front of kids on Tues and Fred knew him — policy holder — so had to go to a Masonic funeral on Thurs. nite and it was depressing so Rogers came over to play bridge and forget about it. On Fri. we stayed home and Sally's Don played piano for us. I ironed and read Mary Webb's The Golden Arrow.

Bill's faults tooth came out on Fri. at school so he has to go to the dentist to get it put in again. He lost it on Sat. doing paper route so had all the kids in the neighbourhood hunt for it and by a lucky miracle Bobby Malcolm found it on the gravel driveway in front of the apartment houses. Bill gave him a quarter but I felt it was hardly enough because it cost $50. in the first place.

Sally is cheer leader again and she got top votes for the publicity manager and the social committee. She chose to run for publicity and won. The teacher said she could easy win either one cause she was way ahead of anyone else. she must be well liked down there at B.C.I. Bill plays rugby — I don't like the idea but he does and Fred does too.

The new people moved in next door with 3 kids and a dog — a big spaniel. If he comes in our yard to GO I'll crown him — turn the hose on him they say, that's the solution — the hose.

Now I must vaccuum rug — The leaves are colouring in front of the house. Come down soon.

Love
Ruby

The Golden Arrow: A novel by Mary Webb.

Sept 22/58

Dear Mother

Haven't any news cept — we were asked to a cottage but it rained so got uninvited and went to the Graham's instead and told them about our trip. They want to go west next year. Maybe we'll go west next year too if all's well. We sure want to go — it's the only time to do it cause the following year Sally will be in grade 13 and that fall she'll be going somewhere to do something else — so like I said, this coming summer we should all go west. Gee it would be fun if Jan and Harry would get a tent and go with us. We could plan where to meet each nite and pitch our tents together and eat and have fun. We'd have to drive hard to do it in 4 weeks but someone we know went out to B.C. and back in 18 days. Wish we had room for you too, mum, would you sleep in a tent? I guess not.

I picked beans for our dinner tonite — Bill is playing football on the Midget team at Orilia. I wish he'd be a bench warmer like he was on the baseball team this summer. Their team won in baseball on Mon. nite so they treated them to ice cream and he said they get a crest but so far he hasn't had his picture taken for the paper as he thought the team would have. Sally took that job on the school paper. She sure likes doing things — as long as she doesn't slip up on her subjects it's all right. She hasn't time to help me with stuff, that's for sure. I don't mind as long as she helps when I ask her to do something.

We'll sure miss you on Thanksgiving and Bill is sick because Tom's not coming. He still wants to play — still not grown up, eh? sh! sh! sh! I don't want him interested in girls — he's getting interested in dancing and is going to a hop at church tonite — I need a new vaccuum so badly — have to kick mine to make motor go.

Come on down later eh? I must make tomato butter before frost gets my tomatoes. Our kids are thrilled about going west — Sally says she'll get more thrilled when we really get going — she can't believe it as yet.

Love
Ruby

Sept 25/58

Dear Jan

Kids are off to school. Fred's still sleeping. He got home late last nite from beyond Aliston with another agent — sold a 10 between them. Very pleased.

Gord Lane, a new agent who owns a hunting lodge summer resort sort of place up past Minden on an Island asked Fred, Jack Moss and his father-in-law and other agents to go up on a duck hunting and fishing week-end — so they're all going up this aft. They'll come home sometime Sunday. I don't want Fred to go but he's never been on a hunt and he wants to try it. He's getting a gun from Bert Loney — Bert borrowed Bill's red cap so Fred went to get it back to wear it and Bert said he'd lend Fred his gun. Fred was the only one who didn't have a gun — I wish it would rain all week-end then they'd stay in and play cards. I know they'll drink — though Gord said Jack's father-in-law doesn't drink much but to me at his daughter's wedding he looked drunk.

Gosh there's so much to do around here — I lie awake nites thinking of stuff — cellar and garage have to be cleaned and garden brought in and the house hasn't been touched all week — I must clean it and the mending is beyond me and I've material to make a skirt and I've no winter hat and Sally needs a new coat and mine needs drycleaning and my hair needs a perm.

Fred's in the tub now — I want him to wear his old ski pants but he won't — says they have to carry stuff into camp — it's on an island — gosh I'll worry till he gets home again. I hate him to go — shooting's so dangerous — people always get killed — he has to take a sleeping bag — I sewed in 2 Indian blankets and a flannellette sheet and it's all ready now. If only it would really really rain.

Have Kay and Dave gone on their trip? Gosh — 25 years married. Jack Moss's father and mother-in-law just had their 25th last month so he must be almost closer in age to the dad and mother then to his wife, eh? Jack's 37 or 38 and Gail is 23 or 21 — no one seems to know. Jack always felt he was too old — said to us did we think he was too old for her. Well I bet he fights with her — he sure bosses her and he does what he likes and always will. Only married two months and he's going on a hunting trip. Is that a happy marriage? I guess not.

Love Ruby

Dear Jan

I worked like a feen when Fred was away. Made tomato butter, finished pickles. Is mother on her trip? Where did she go? I dug up plants one morning, put 7 tulip bulbs in a pot for next Easter and brought in tomatoes, peeled a basket of apples and made apple betty and picked apples off tree and made apple sauce and ironed. I just kept going all day long — didn't even stop to watch ball game on TV.

Haven't done anything about trip as yet — Ron Hade brought our communion cards and he's going west next year — I bet there'll be scads going west. I hope we can start in June — hope Sally's departmentals won't hold us up. She's taking 10 subjects — what is Judy doing?

On Sunday kids went to Sunday School — Sally teaching her 8 year olds. Bill came home after to study then went off to play golf with the boys. Rogers asked us for supper but we didn't go cause we expected Fred home from his hunting trip and he did come at 5. I made mince pie to welcome him home but he ate so much rich food up north that he wasn't hungry — didn't even drink tea or coffee for supper. Guess the cook at camp was too generous with butter when he fried fish, they caught 9 which they ate — Fred caught 2. They killed 3 fish-eating ducks which they didn't eat. Meat balls and spagetti one nite and steaks — he said he had a good time, said it was quite a weekend — played poker and won 80¢ — he said. He didn't shoot, only fished — it was pretty cold. He took ski pants and wore them over other pants and Dave's old jacket — I bet he was cold but he said no.

Well it's all under the bridge, all over and forgotten. He's home safe.

On Monday I washed — Bill needed pants. With mother and Kay away why don't you all come down here this weekend? Fred has to count collection and Sally will be in Toronto for weekend to a Hi Y convention — Judy could go out with her beau. Fred says tell them to come so we can discuss our route through the states next summer; leaves are turning so it will be nice driving.

Oh kid, we're still going west with you. Sanfransisco here we come — sure are saving money for it. Come down, come down.

Love Ruby

Departmentals: End of year examinations set by the Department of Education in Ontario.

Sept. 30/58

Dear Jan

We went up passed Orilia to a cottage for supper last nite on Lake Simcoe — Dad and I paddled round a big island that took us 3/4 of an hour and I'm sorta stiff this morning. Kay would like to go on our trip too. They should get a tent and take mother — then we'd all be on the road — can't you just see us all tripping?

You should come down here to look at tents. We think you should get a tent rather then a station wagon. A wagon would be ok but what about dressing and undressing in it and where to put bags when the beds are out and how can you all four sleep in a station wagon? Like Fred says, you can't really move around and the bother of covering the windows so no one sees you would be a problem. I would suggest you get a Chev — 1958 are beauties — and put tent and things inside like we did. No rack on top — a nuisance and bother. Only thing you need is 4 sleeping bags $12.95 each, 4 sleeping air mattresses $11.95 or cheaper — a tent like ours at $89.00 if you get it on sale — otherwise it's $127.00 and a bag to keep it in $6. Clothes for 4 weeks — you can wash out underwear. What does mother think of us going west? Gee I hope it works out ok. We must get dope on it all, maps and plans —

Guess what? There are only 12 boys on the senior rugby team, all the others have broken ribs, arms, legs or figures or such. Now tonite Bill said Sally's beau has a broken rib — or thinks so — had to go to the doctor to see — so that's another one off — gosh I wish Bill didn't play rugby.

Sally's baby-sitting from 6.30 to 11 tonite — another dame phoned too to have her sit Fri and Sat. Gosh I'm stiff and I have a sore spot on my leg — looks like a bruise. There are special events on TV this week and I forgot to turn it on till now — I must watch a fashion show — — beans — I've mist 20 minutes of it. Now it's over — no, I don't think so — my new ladies home journal and the story of Peter Townsend and Princess Margaret is in it — Peter's close friend wrote the story and says they're still in love. Must read it.

Come on down eh? Our kids are thrilled about going west, are yours?

Love, Ruby

Oct. 10/58

Dear Jan

I've ten minutes to write you then off to work. We got a card from Mother, a polar bear in the Rochester zoo. She said no shopping for her, she was terribly tired. I hope Maude isn't making her go and go and shop and shop. She said they might get here soon, I'm hoping they come tonite — it's so wet and lousy out. I'd like them to stay here and have mother rest up.

Leaves are sure coming off trees — I got Fred to put storms on yesterday and glad I did. So often he's put them on in the rain or snow or cold weather and yesterday was a beautiful day even though they are getting splashed with rain today I like getting snugged in for the winter. I planted bulbs this week — so that's done. I hope squirrels don't eat them. I found some peanuts hid in the flower bed. I brought in my plants — one of those patient plants and ivey and a green leaf with yellow, that's all, and I must get a purple plant from Kath, a funny one, and I have a white geranium. I don't want any more. I never have luck with houseplants — I forget to water them.

Sally hopes to buy a new skirt and a horsehair crinoline in Toronto, I can hardly wait to see what she brings home and what fun she had. I bet they'll spend 1/2 their time on street cars and subways, getting to and from places. And I bet she spent the $22 I gave her. She's letting her hair grow again, she wishes she'd never had it cut. All the boys said they didn't like it so she's letting her pony tail grow again and is impatient about it.

We're only on phoning list of square dancing if they need an extra couple. We're tired of it and would rather play bridge. Costs more this year too. I've talked to people who lived out in B.C. they've a tax on things — 5¢ on $1.

Sally had her name on the front page of our paper and she was on TV in Toronto — did you see her?

Must go now, Fred's ready.

Love, Ruby

Dear Jan

Mother arrived Sun. nite — just when we were eating off the bones of a 20 lb. turkey. She's reading now and Maude is ironing. Bill and Sally are doing homework. Both are sick about Ronnie Henderson and Rob Beachman who were killed over the weekend — you remember Ronnie — Judy went out with him last 24th of May. They were driving along the river road — going fast or something — and turned upside down and both were killed. 3 boys in car ahead we think were racing them — though they claim the boys were going only 40 miles an hour — they knocked over 6 posts and turned upside down in 4 feet of water on Sunday nite around 9. They were found too late — dead — can't understand why or how they died. We knew both boys — Rob you met here — he used to golf with Bill. We've driven him in and out so often to the club. He's a honey and so was Ronnie. Double funeral today — kids both went — they slept very little last nite — Sally heard it in Toronto and the convention was spoilt for them. We drove out to see where they were killed and it just seemed unbelievable to see the spot — a straight road too — they must have gone fast — both only 16. Rob was the only son and his mother is in hospital with pneaumonia. Ronnie is an only son too, Enough of that. My Bill is so upset he had me sleep with him last nite, he was so restless, we talked for ages then he got to sleep after 2 aspirins. Sally was sick to her stomach and so white I came downstairs with her, she nearly had a fit when we went to the funeral home — 2 coffins in one room and scads of flowers.

Ronnie's parents square danced with us — they're nice. Poor souls. The Beachmans we didn't know. The whole of Barrie Collegiate practically went to the funeral.

Mother will go home on Thursday, Maude had her hair done today. We're going to play bridge tonite. Rogers came over last nite, I washed just before they came and hung stuff outside after they were here at nite and it didn't dry very well — glad I did — cause this morning I just seemed to visit with Mother and Maude.

Bill sneezed just now. I must iron, this is just to let you know we're having fun. I'll write later.

Love Ruby

Oct. 29/58

Dear Kay

I hope you can read this, I'm lying on studio watching Front Page Challenge. Girl at store and myself are betting to see who can lose 5 lbs in 2 weeks — both of us are too fat and we need to get thin. I'm about 112 and she's a 16 or 18 and wants to get into a 16 or 14. I want to get down to 107 or 5. Want to join us? We haven't priced the bet yet.

Haven't much to say. Jan and Harry are all excited about trip west. Isn't their new car gorgeous? I love the color. Gosh — now we're planning to be off to Los Angeles — not just San Fransisco. Boy I wonder if we'll ever get there — 4 weeks seems so short for so far but still look at all the countries you go to see in 2 months in Europe so I guess we can make it.

I should iron, my washing is damped. Fred knows the chap from Aliston who has a second winner ticket in the Irish sweep stakes, nice eh? He's a policy holder of Fred's and an owner of school buses which pass here every day. He's not poor, Fred says lucky guy. He looked at his ticket and the date on it was over so he thought it wasn't any good any more and put it in the garbage that was suppose to be collected on Monday but he forgot to put the can out for the garbage man to empty. By Thursday it was getting pretty high and he decided to take it to the dump and empty it himself and he did and that same day he got a notice that he had a horse that was running. Boy was he excited. He had to have the ticket to get the money if he won any so he went out to the dump and looked where his garbage was and sure enough he found it. That's how close he was to losing $60,000. But if he hadn't forgotten his garbage on Monday he wouldn't have had it at all.

Wanted to say something else about this but now I forget what it was. I was entreeg by lady docker on TV. Kids are studying, Fred's out. Tonite's the store Haloween party but we're not going. Fred never goes to such things. Bill joined drama club at school, has a small part in a play. Football practise is over for this year — I'm glad and he's not playing hockey — only skiing. He's so nuts about that I'm afraid when he's on his own he's going to go somewhere where they have more snow all the time so he can ski and ski. Sally's through cheer leading too for the winter. She finds German hard. Well I guess that's all,

Love, Ruby

Dear Mum

Haven't any news. We were asked to go square dancing but we're not going — too old or something. Sally got a new dress. It's a red and grey and black plad. I like it and so does she and everyone else — Fri. she'll wear it for the first time in public and with her hair cut. No more pony tail; she just got it long enough to do it up nicely when off it came again. Mine's growing but I don't think I'll leave it grow — maybe till Xmas to see what you all think but I'm not sure I like it — makes me look older and it's still not long enough to do up.

I get 20% off at the store this month but haven't much money to buy stuff. Sally's dress cost 19.95, her coat 39.00 — not that I paid for them — but I'm saving for our trip west.

Nothing new — no one seems to be shopping — people haven't money — it's really terrible — we're always under at the store — all the departments aren't selling what they sold last year. People just aren't in the stores, they haven't the money to buy — too many out of work.

Kay just phoned and said she and Dave were going to come down this week-end. Boy we're thrilled; they haven't been here for ages and we're dying to have Sally's beau and Dave play together on the piano. Don won the cup for the best rugby player. He's atheletic too — not just musical, see.

Now I'd best get going, I do want to wash curtains in living room and diningroom so they'll be clean for Kay and Dave. Boy are we glad they're coming, wish you all were too. Haven't we had nice weather? Santa Clause parade is here this Sat. I hope business will pick up after, paper was full of store sales this weekend. The ski place Bill wanted to go to in Quebec burnt down yesterday.

Dave is going to bring his music and Kay is bringing limburger cheese and summer sausage.

Love
Ruby

Jan. 8/59

Dear Mum

I'm waiting for Fred to come for lunch. I must take a little time to do some drawing. Just had a call from Muriel Conner — she had us in for Sunday supper long ago and I haven't had her in since — must do that some time soon. I always feel terrible not having her when ever I see her. Sally's taking vitamin pills.

I have to sew stick for blind in kitchen — I should go out for some fresh air too — I never go out when I'm home from now till Easter'ness I have to. I'm lazy, I guess, just lazy.

Christmas trees are all gone now. Garbage picked them up this morning. There's a full moon coming on your birthday. Fred got a new suit today — it's nice — dark blue and grey stripe. He's got a light one and needs a dark one badly. Came home at noon with coat to see if I like it on him.

Bill got his report — 63% — he's not too happy, wishes he'd get 75. He's working harder now, works alone, Sally gets dad to help her but Bill only asks for help with his maths.

Sally went up to the hospital with about 35 girls to go through the hospital and nurses resident. She thinks now she might like to be a nurse — not the nursing type but a specialist in lab stuff, that means 3 years to train, then a year specializing at Toronto University or somewhere. These poor kids don't know what they want to be but school teaching is out she says, yet she loves her Sunday School class.

Now I'd best get going, I feed birds and squirrels — they always look for food. I give them 1 to 3 or 4 pieces of bread. Squirrel will take a whole piece if I put it out whole, I've been cutting it up in wee pieces otherwise sparrows don't get any, this way they can carry it away with them cause they're afraid of the squirrel.

Take care of yourself. Here's Fred.

Love, Ruby

Dear Jan

How are the stories — are you trying? Get going kid, I keep making them up in my head but never get them written. I want to get out my rug this morning to see what I can do about putting it together. I'm going to get it done this winter or bust.

Haven't drawn anything lately. Ollie Mitchell's pictures that she painted are hanging in her livingroom — copied off old calenders — I'm sure. Those types where the full moon is shining on snow and a creek and a garden with an English cottage — you know that kind. Not for me. I don't want to paint that way. I like Harry's stuff. I like the free bold strokes — own expression etc etc. Not that stuff that looks copied. Say that one book is terrific — course in beginning watercolor painting — it's $3.95, I'd like to own it. It says, "the world's foremost musicians are not above practising a composition over and over again, so why shouldn't a pictorial artist practise the melodies and harmonies he will use in his own compositions?" I haven't finished reading it — I got lots out of it — now to put it all into practise. I must re-read it too so it will sink in.

Bill's getting a ride to school with Joe — it's so icey. There goes Danny to take Sue's Rolf to school, he does it every morning — poor kid never has any fun with other kids — they get him and take him to kindergarten every day.

Fred's getting up now — having a bath. "Do not fear the stigma of being corny." Has Harry read this book? Get it for him at the library.

Happy birthday to Kay today. Lucky her going to Mexico — wish I could say my husband's bought tickets to fly to Mexico from 6 to 27th of March. Gosh wouldn't it be wonderful to have money like that? It's not a shame to be poor but money sure would be welcome. Oh kid, save for the trip west, eh? We must go. Ches and Mabel talk as if Fred speaks to them that he's not going. Such a shame. Mabel said this week — Ruby's trying to talk Fred into going west. I didn't think I was at all — he seemed just as keen as me and never says we're not — though neither of us have done any writing away for maps — have you? Must do it one of these days and too I must try for a lisence — license — how do you spell it? I'm listening to a minister on radio as well as writing this.

Love
Ruby

Dear Jan

Kay phoned about mother — gosh, isn't that terrible — how is she? You know when I think of it now — she made odd little remarks such as about her will — and Fred heard her say she wondered if this would be the last Christmas that we'd all be together etc. So you can see now she must have been thinking and worrying a lot, eh? I hope she's ok. Write me eh? I'll send $5 for flowers and you spend what you like. You can buy tulips at Loblaws or the A and P to take up or what you want — Loblaws here had 10 tulips for 69¢. It would cost me about $3 or so to send flowers from here and they wouldn't be any nicer. You could take them when you go up to see mother — unless you don't like the idea.

Did I ever give you those hollyhock seeds — if not I guess they've been thrown out. I can't find them. Those bulbs are up about 2 inches — I'm trying to keep them in the dark and to make them grow slowly. They say many many roots are the secret of bulbs. So I'm trying to root them. So far they're still yellow with a very light shade of green at tips and white at the ground. They are growing — by Easter — just Feb and 22 days away — they may be blooming. I'm busting to see the ones I planted outside too. I hope squirrels won't eat them — I try to feed them so they won't be hungry.

I'm going to the Dr. to see about my spine — or near it — it's sore when I sit down — I fell in the spring — guess it was spring or early fall — on patio — I told Kay and she said she remembered me writing or telling her I fell and then I got thinking yes she was right, I did fall and fall hard, I even lay there for a second or so before I got up — but I can't remember when — spring or fall. Must have a bath — will write later to tell you Dr's report. Must be there at 3.

Hi — I'm ok. Says it's from fall; only a local thing caused from pressure — had a long name but I can't remember it. Said heat might help — sitting up straight — not to slump — nothing to worry — gave me pills for nerves and for hot flashes.

Fred's going to mail this — must go — I made Fred take me to a show last nite to forget about mum, I felt so badly — Dr. said today her age is with her and she'll be ok — he said not to worry, she'll be ok.

Love Ruby

Dear Kay

How's mum — better for having it all over, I'm sure she'll be ok. My Dr. said she will — says old age cancer doesn't grow. Look at Chester's mother — they gave her 2 months to live after her operation and she's still here 2 years later and feeling wonderful — she's spending the day here with me tomorrow. I hope mum gets along ok. Jan said she was pretty frisky for having an operation the day before but that was probably her nerves. We'll come home when she's better unless you want and need me. Let me know.

I'm listening to Fighting Words on TV. I'm going to send in a quotation I read in an art book, "an artist is not a man who gives the public what it wants, he is a man who makes the public want what he gives it."

I'm reading the Klondike story in Maclean's right now too — do you think Mother would remember anything about the Klondike? She must have been around 15 or so, eh?

Bill went skiing in the rain and got all wet. He's learning to jump, a chap is teaching him and 2 other kids. He's so keen. He's dreaming of being Canada's Junior champion and going to the Olympics, etc.

Sally taught at public school yesterday — watched a teacher teach and taught arithmetic herself to a class — she seemed to enjoy it but I really didn't get all the details. I guess I went to bed too early — she was upstairs studying when we came home. She got good marks — in geography 81, in maths 89. She says she didn't do too well though, said her percent was only 70. But we'll see when reports are out.

Fred's out working. He's thrilled cause a chap phoned and is going to take a $20,000 tomorrow, nice eh?

We might get a private line cause we've a party line who talks all the time — more then I do — I can never get the line and no one can get me. I've had people say they've tried for 3 days to get us.

How's the diet? Are you thinner? We've eaten all the Xmas chocolates so now I'm trying to lay off sweets. We're having sauerkraut today.

Haven't any news — this is just prattle. Wish I were nearer so I could go to see mother — write and let me know how she is. Thanks for phoning me. Take care of yourself.

Love, Ruby

Feb. 4/59

Dear Kay

Thanks so much for the lovely meal. Mabel was fascinated with all your interesting things from your trips. She wants to try making the soup and so do I — it was super. Thanks for the meat and the bread. Bill was extremely thrilled for it — he ate the summer sausage immediately we got home at 9 oclock. It was such a lovely sunny day and one just felt like driving so I was glad Chester took me up on my Let's keep on going till we get to London. Mabel was glad we went too, not cross at Ches, only happy for me to get home to see mother. Chester felt badly that I didn't get a longer visit with her or stop to buy her something but we just kept going to get there before visiting hours were over and we wanted to see Jan and you and Mabel's friend. We had so much fun. Mabel said everything was so different and so good and she said you were so nice — not a bit high hat — so natural. She enjoyed it. Many many thanks. They both loved your homes and she wants to have flowers across her window like Jan's.

Today is Chester's birthday and we're having a surprise party for him on Sat. in the Hade's cellar — they've an empty reck room and it's decorated with streamers from a party for their 7 year old. Chester has never had a party in his life because his young brother was killed on his birthday in the last war and his mother always cries all day. So Mabel says. Chester is so good to her, he's so good natured anyway, cept he's a riot in his own way — odd at times in his ideas — but we enjoy him and he sure is good to me.

I thought mother looked well, no change in her since Xmas. I hope I didn't upset her popping in and out. My old heart sure beat a mighty fast beat when I went in to see her. Hope her's was ok.

We have a private telephone line now — 90¢ more — noone could get me in the morning. Now I must go — I want to shovel snow before Fred comes home — it's so nice out. Did you like my hair do? Wasn't it fun yesterday? I wish I could do that more often. Give mum my best.

Love, Ruby

Dear Kay

Dot Walton, a girl from the store and her son 5 are coming over this aft to eat cookies. I baked some yesterday and used basic recipe — shortening, brown sugar, egg, vanilla, baking powder and flour — that idea and then I added dates to some, nuts to others, new carmel chips, raisins, spice and peanut butter to the rest so I have six different kinds. They're not bad. Wished I'd had some coconut too.

I made bread on Sat. Mixed it Fri. nite and let it stand then at 5.30 Sally woke up, couldn't sleep, came downstairs and I heard her, so I got up and put bread in pans. I used all whole wheat flour and no white — is that right? And you didn't tell me how long to bake it or at what temperature. I just guessed and Fred felt that though I had it in an hour it wasn't baked long enough so I put it back in. I found the yeast settled at the bottom of my pot when I went to put the dough on flour to knead — it seemed awful wet and I had to use lots of flour to knead it — my hands were terribly doughy. What did I do wrong?

Well Dot isn't here yet so I'll keep writing — I'm taking red pills for heat — I sure like these — the others didn't help me one speck — these are 10 days take — 10 days don't. I'm at the don't stage. I still wake up in the nite but I'm not steaming. Gosh I'm sure my blood was boiling. I got so hot I told the Dr. I'd like to go outside in the back yard and lie down in the snow with nothing on — I bet I'd melt all the snow in the garden. He said save that energy and use it on his icy driveway. But these pills are helping. I'm glad I'm taking them. I was so uncomfortable and terrible, now I'm not and I can get stuff done and I feel like doing things too — I washed a huge wash this morning and this aft I tidied up for Dot and tore some stuff for rug — last rug I'll ever make, that's for sure.

I guess I'll get out 2 cups and a glass for milk for Dot's little boy, it's 3 oclock and they should be here soon. I knitted Sally some white mitts to go with the scarf you gave her. Sue next door gave her a brown spotted wool skirt, size 10 and too small for Sue. Nice eh? How's mother, is she home? Here's Dot now.

Love, Ruby

Feb. 6/59

Dear Jan

It's snowing — Bill will love that. He used his new skis at the hill yesterday — they go like the wind, he says. I hope he doesn't kill himself one of these days. Like that chap in Germany and one chap here yesterday who broke a bone in his foot that came right thro and he bleed and bleed. Bill said it was terrible — but thank goodness he missed it all — chap and his friend were skiing on north hill alone — just the 2 of them — and this happened. Their truck was up on the hill — the other chap carried his pal bleeding almost to death to the truck — and had a hang of a time getting it started and then he rushed him to the ski spot where 3 doctors looked after him and rushed him to meet the ambulance to go to hospital. They put a turiqnine — one of those things — on him — too bad the guy didn't do it at the hill right away — but gosh, one never thinks in these terrible times.

That's enough of such miserable thoughts. Did I ever tell you the Balls were in Barrie for a ski meet in January? Out of the blue I asked them if they'd like to come to our house — I said we'd like to have them if they'd like to keep out of the cold or such and they said no thanks they were at a motel and would be ok and warm. But Mrs. Ball said to Bill he was to tell me they were sorry they didn't get in to see me. Whee I'm glad they didn't. I really had the house in a mess with my rug — but any way I did my duty and asked them. I guess I'd have died if they'd really have come. I didn't think of what I'd do with them till after they said no thank you. Guess we'd have given them our Xmas liquor but I never even thought of that. I never saw them again cause I didn't go to the jump the next day. Their son told Bill they're coming up thro the lakes this summer with their 3 boats — touring the whole lake system. He said will you be here and Bill said no, we're going to California and the son said for how long and Bill said a month. But he said give us a dingle if he came here cause we might be back by the time they come. Bill said that really set him back. No he didn't do it to be snooty — it only sounded that way to us.

Here's our mail man — no letter from home — to let me know how Mother is — hope she's ok. Please be carefull. Do you want me home? Let me know.

Love Ruby

Dear Kay

Sally is asking kids here for punch before a big formal dance at school on Friday. We rented a punch bowl for $1 and glasses for 2¢ each. She has a list of 50 she owes or wants but they won't all come. We're going to serve ginger ale and cider — if we can get it — going to sample it first to make sure it's not hard. I only hope the 50 don't all come at once — that's too many coats to pile on one bed. We borrowed a toilet seat so Fred could paint ours — it's drying now. I'm trying to clean up our old floors — it's quite a task — we perhaps should have gotten a man with a sander to do it — the finish is off in the used spots.

Sally seems to have gotten good marks — second highest in some subjects — spelling is her worst enemy, she said they took 7, 8 and 10 marks off. She still goes with Don but I haven't seen him to talk to since Dec. 30. He never comes cept to bring her to the door and off again. Last Fri. he came in but I was in bed. Next year he goes to Toronto University. Don't know what will happen to them then. I don't know what to do about this going steady business. They say it's not good at their age but Sally seems to be the steady kind. Look at how fond she is of dad. Quite a few boys seemed to like her and ask her out before she went steady but she always seems to end up with just one — Murray for a year and now Don. They're nice boys and I don't see any harm in it really — better I'd say then running around with all kinds who try her out and want to neck and maybe make her turn into a tough little type.

Look at how we were — we had plenty of beaus and yet we always had sort of a steady hanging around. Remember how Ken Knowlton and Buzz Antler and Chuck and those kids were always down at the house and even when we had a date with somebody else they'd be there and talk to you or mum or each other while I'd go out to the show with somebody new. Those were the days, kid, kids nowdays don't know what they're missing by getting stuck with one boy when they're Just in their teens. But what can one do about it — it seems to be the way of the world. The girls who don't go steady miss out on parties and never know where they're at. All those coming to Sally's party will be steadies.

Well I must get at my floors.

Love, Ruby

Feb. 10/59

Dear Kay

The party is over and if I do say so myself the house really looked clean and lovely. I cleaned windows and mirrors and Fred got my mirror in the dressing table fixed for $5. — was I ever happy with that — and he bought me a bouquet of red tulips and then what a disappointment! Those kids didn't eat a thing. Sally wanted something different than what everybody else has — just fruit juice and potato chips — she said they'll eat lots and was worried there'd not be enough. She made us buy loaves and loaves of all kinds of bread, 3 cherry loaves, 3 chop suey loaves — they cut into 20 pieces — I made a pineapple raison bread, Fred bought 3 date breads that cut into 12 slices — 39¢ at Woolworth's — we buttered it all and guess what they ate? FIVE slices of bread. Besides that she had to have 1 lb. of bridge mix, 1 lb. of peanuts, and grapes, and 3 bags of potato chips 39¢ a bag — and a big big box of them besides and 2 different kinds of potato dip and ritz biscuits and pretzel sticks. She said they'd all drink 2 or 3 glasses of punch and we'd have to keep filling the bowl. They ate practically nothing and less then one bowl of punch. It was so disappointing, Fred and I felt terrible. The party could have cost us no more then $5 and it did cost well over $15. And we were left with all that bread to eat up and we couldn't possibly do it before it got stale so we gave it away and Bill took some to the ski chalet to give to the kids. And we still have plenty left and all that gingerale and juice.

30 kids came and Sally said they had a wonderful time. Fred and I think they don't know what a wonderful time is. We decided the party is only to show off the girl's dresses and corsages — they expect to have new dresses each time. The girls buy the boys butineers, white carnations for buttonholes — truly Fred and I nearly died — they sat around like show pieces — Fred said — each was trying to outdo the other in posing. We never saw the like — old crowneys — they looked so silly — sitting or standing not talking — never laughing or having fun — just like old people watching each other. It was like hawk watching hawk — don't you dare look at my girl or talk to my girl and my girl don't you dare look at any other boy or talk to them. At the dance I suppose it's you dance with me only — they're all steadys. Really! I don't think they have any fun. And besides the expense of the party I got a hair-do $2. Can't save for our trip if I go on like that.

Love
Ruby

Dear Kay

   Sally's Don came here again on Sat. night to eat bread left from the party. Before he came I heard Sally talk to him on the phone — at the dance she seemed to want to trade dances and he was afraid to or she didn't want to and when he did she didn't like it — or what — I didn't get all they were talking about — couldn't hear his side on the phone, ding it, but they seemed to be arguing or something. They sure don't have the fun we had when we were kids.

   We took the Rogers to see Bill ski on Sunday — boy I wish you could see him. He's terrific — not that the others aren't too but he goes up tow and down hill in about two minutes. The hill was and is so fast — all ice. One chap broke his shin bone while we were there — if you can't turn and stop you've had it. Coming down hill full speed — and I mean speed — and what a hill!!!! You have to know how. The hill is a hill — not a little bitty one and now with all this snow it's bigger then ever. Really dangerous if you aren't careful. Only the best skiers use it and Bill even waxed his skis to go faster. I'm glad I don't go out often to see him, I'd be too afraid. Not so much since he got his $85 skis cause they have steel edges so sharp they cut your hand so he can cut into ice and stop right in front of you. He's really good — Mr. Bruke, the coach, said he's a natural. He's so nuts about it and so happy.

   Well that's enough of Bill and his skiing and Sally and her party — both kids are sure different — I think more and more Sally is like Fred — she never tells you a thing — when you ask she thinks I'm nosey — guess teenagers are like that — but if you don't ask they think you don't care. Bill will talk all day about skiing — if you ask him and talk to him. He's like me. And Sally like her dad — yet she gets excited and is she ever a worry wort.

   Here's the milk man. The snow is so high on the road you can barely see the tops of the cars as they pass. Haven't seen so much snow since I was a kid. I love it.

   Are you and Jan mad at me — you haven't written for so long or what?

                              Love, Ruby

Dear Mum

Sally was cross at me Sat. cause I said she was running after Don — dad felt she was too. Mad at me too cause I told her to count ten before she lost her temper — she was cross at Don cause he asked her to a show then phoned up and said he was going to it with his boy friend and would call for her at 9.30 to take her to a party — an invitation house party. She phoned him up (1st time I know of) cause she thought he was home alone — his parents were suppose to be in Toronto but they didn't go cause mother was afraid of Friday 13th; the mother answered the phone so had Don call Sally back. Sally was furious and said it was important for him to call right away, I saw her face how cross she was and I said "maybe he hasn't got money to get a hair cut and take you to a show too" — he bought her Moir's Pot of Gold chocolates — 1 lb box and they're expensive. She got so mad at me cause I said she was running after him that she wouldn't eat — she never eats when she's upset. She doesn't sleep either — I worry about her — but I guess I shouldn't — well then that was all. Fri. and Sat she wouldn't talk to me — stayed in her room — ate her lunch in the livingroom while Bill and I ate in the kitchen. Dad got home late. All morning and afternoon I ignored her — except calling up to her to hear something on the radio and calling her to the phone etc. Then her boy friend came and I called her — no answer — she had her door locked — I tried to get in her room — she opened it and went down to see him. I said your girl friend's not talking to me — she got cross and then what happened or what was said I don't remember but she told me why don't you go away, we can get along without you!!!!

That's what really hurt me. I told her I'd been thinking of it lately and just didn't know where I wanted to go — to Alaska or Spain cause it's cheap living there or to Mexico or where? I was just waiting to get a little more money in the bank. Fred was reading the funny paper. He didn't open his mouth. And that's what hurt most of all — his silence.

So that's how it all started, all week and since the new year she's been telling me off — it was the same when I asked what and if she got a valentine from Don — it was none of my business and she didn't even show me the box of chocolates he gave her. Then at nite after dinner while Fred and I were having tea she whispered to him — then she and Fred did the dishes — I was writing a letter and she said, She's telling granny all about me. I guess the truth hurt her — she told a white lie — cause she said she didn't mean it about me going away — was only kidding. Didn't sound like kidding to me after not speaking to me all morning and afternoon. Anyway when Fred and I talked I talked loudly I guess, not shouting, just talking out loud, and Sally heard us and came downstairs, asked if we were fighting. Dad said no, she was to get to bed. Then she broke down and said she was sorry she fought with me and she kissed us and said she didn't want to fight any more and said she wouldn't trade either of us and said all her friends fight with one or the other parent — Connie and her dad, Patsy and her mother and Don and his dad — she didn't want to fight any more and please let's be like we use to be — we didn't fight so let's not fight any more cause she hated it.

It's true mum, we never use to fight — it's all happened so sudden; Fred being so silent — it got me down.

Bill didn't even know we had a fight — he was skiing on Sat. and on Sun. nite he was asleep and didn't hear us ironing it out.

Anyway it's all over and Sally helps me with the dishes and is her old self again. She really is a good kid.

Should we buy a felt rug for under our livingroom one — costs about $18 and they say they wear longer if you've one underneath — nice time to think of it after it's been on the floor for at least 5 years, eh?

Love, Ruby

Feb. 23/59

Dear Mum

I feel terrible about that long phone call. It will cost you a fortune. Please let me pay towards it at least. I wish you would — I couldn't get to sleep for thinking how much it will be.

I didn't tell Fred you called. I believe like Mabel said — Fred is jealous of you and Jan and Kay too — cause I'm always talking about you three. I knew he didn't like me always saying this and that and from now on I won't. I didn't know he cared so much — I won't even let him mail all my letters to you now or read all yours to him. I truly think Mabel's right — he's jealous. Why? Cause he thinks I like my family better than him — jealous cause Kay and Jan and you have more money — why? I'm not sure but I bet he's jealous and he's never let on — only by silence — and I didn't even notice it. Anyway whatever it is, whatever it was, he's nice to me again and always kisses me goodbye, talks and is his nice old self again even though he hasn't a lot of money. Maybe it hurts him too to see me work and Kay and Jan not, and yet he knows working makes me happier cause I'm busy and too it's true I would hate to be running to teas and stuff all the time. I really like working only I don't like spending my money. I'd like to save it. However I'm not spending it on things he should be paying for — only a little now and then — since Xmas I've truly been saving. He pays kids $2 for meals at school — I used to help but I don't now. I'll see if my not spending makes him work harder. He paid for the mirror for my dressing table today. Don't worry about him, mum, he said he liked you better then he ever did. Said he's getting to know and understand you better — but mum, please don't worry over me. I'll not let either of them hurt me again. We're all happy again here, so don't worry, we had it out night before last. Talked it over so all's well. We got our differences off our chest and I sure feel better. I was all for leaving this place and never coming back. Bill was the only one holding me here. But all's well. Don't say anything in your letters, eh?

Well I must get at my floors, I'm cleaning them with lestoil. Please let me pay for the phone call — please. I'd be happier. Fred didn't know we talked. Don't mention it.

Love, Ruby

Dear Jan

Sally and I went to the Presbyterian church to hear her Don play the organ while the organist was away. That's pretty good eh for a 17 year old? He did pretty well — made some mistakes but he knew we were there and I think that made him scared too but he should get over that if he intends to play in public. He plays at Kawanis festivals and he plays the piano while the organist plays in their own church. So I doubt if Sally and I scared him. The organ and leading the choir and just playing by himself for the whole church frightened him and he's always afraid, he says. He did ok — only played so slow — but a Presbyterian told me that's how their own organist plays all the time so I guess she told Don not to rush thro the hymns. The church is a new modern one — all light wood and all windows — but oh my — what noisy kids — never heard such a noisy church — no carpet and it's terrible — the minister was poor — read his sermon and prayers and seemed so nervice — it was such an unrelaxed church as far as reverence goes relaxed yes — to the extent of racket — you could talk out loud or do what you like — the kids did it all the time and lucky not many people were at it — or it would have been worse.

I met Don's grandfather — he was there. His dad I saw too for the first time, waiting to drive Don and gramp home. Gramp is short as I am and really friendly and nice, the dad I only saw behind the car wheel — he looks very serious. Don's mother is up visiting in Toronto at a brother's house. Guess she gets tired washing and ironing for 3 men and likes to talk to her brother's wife.

Sally just came downstairs and I asked her what Don's gramp said about me after church when I talked to him. She said he told Don's father, "Sally's mother is a young looking woman" — but he didn't hear a word I said. He's stone deaf.

Love Ruby

Dear Mother

The most wonderful thing has happened to Bill—least he thinks so and we think it's nice for him but are not too sure if it's a good idea though we gave him our ok and the principal when we phoned him said, "Well we don't like to see him out of school but if you say ok, ok, he can catch up when he comes back."

Bill has been asked by the Brukes to go to Mt. Tremblant, Que. and to Stowe Vermont for skiing for a week. He's so thrilled. They have a boy 10 who's taking a boy his age along, and Linda, 13, asked Bill—at the ski club she trails him like a puppy. The Brukes like him and say he's a good skiier. They're taking our 2 sleeping bags and air mattresses and a lunch—they sleep at a friend's in Montreal, get up early Sat. and go to Stowe to ski till Sun. then back to the friend's overnite—friend's an ex hockey star with girls 15 and 17 and they're going to Stowe too. Then the Brukes take the 6 of them on Monday to Mt. Tremblant. The people who own the cabin in the mountains are other friends of the Brukes and they'll use their cabin till Fri. The Brukes cook breakfast, have a snack at the clubhouse and big dinner there at nite. This is Mr. Bruke's winter holiday. They went last year without the children, missed them so much they decided to take them and 2 others to share the wonderful time. Nice eh? Bill has to pay for his tows, meals out and his hotel at Stowe, but we feel it's cheap compared with going himself or with friends. He's taking school books along and will study at nite for an hour or so—all his teachers said they'd give him homework to do.

We feel this trip won't hurt him socially—the Brukes are nice people—he's Dutch, she's Canadian, they don't drink. She's darling and he's deaf. They love kids. Would you have let him go? He's paying for the trip out of his paper route money. We just felt we couldn't miss it for him. He talks mountains all the time and here's his chance. I've his clothes all washed and ready to go—Brukes like having Bill around—say he's a good kid and a big help. He's so happy—I'm glad for him. It's a wonderful experience for him.

Brukes said Bill shouldn't break a leg now—he's too good a skiier to get into trouble that way. They expect to be gone 8 days—want to try out different places in the Laurentians. Bill is so thrilled. Will write later to tell you about dining room rugs.

Love Ruby

Dear Kay

Sally went to Toronto this aft with a gang and a teacher to see University and industries and different places to give kids ideas as to what to go through for after Grade 13. She's happy too — wonderful experience for her. She works on Sat. If they didn't work they couldn't go places — and I think it's good for them to work — they realize money takes them places and they couldn't go if they didn't have it. The Hade kids are doing Bill's papers, they said Bill give us half your route. Bill said, No I need the money. He realizes his paper route is his gold mine. Kids at school his age haven't any money, he's really glad he has the route and didn't part with it when in high school. He said I'm hanging on to it. Sally realizes she hasn't any money when she doesn't work at Mussers on Sat. She gave it up after Xmas but she's at it again — but not steady — only now and then. I want them to know they have to work to get things — they don't and can't go here and there if they haven't the money — it's a good lesson. It's not, "Dad I want this and I want that," all the time. Fred did say "Should I put some money in the bank for Bill to pay back what he took out for his trip?" I said, "Wait till he comes home to see how much he spends."

What do you think of this trip? Did we do right or wrong by letting him miss school. Teachers all said they'd help him when he came back. I think it will help him work harder — he knows if his marks hadn't improved on his last report he wouldn't have been allowed to go. Fred said I guess it's part of his education too to live and get along with others and to see things. This might be his only chance to go with the Brukes and they're so nice. We'd never take him to Mt. Tremblant or Stowe because we don't ski.

Well I wonder if we'll get a card from him today. Gosh you never know what fun the kids will have in life — there's Bill — a week's skiing — all out of the blue it happened. Just what he's been dreaming of.

I'm at diningroom rug — want to have it done when Bill comes home — so must do dishes and clean house so I can get at it.

Love
Ruby

Dear Jan

We miss Bill. Sure makes a difference in food — one loaf of bread lasts ages. Haven't any news. Our organist is leaving, she and Rev. Weldon had a fight; this is the 2nd one who's left since we got Weldon — someone said they want to get rid of him now. He didn't get along with the supply minister either.

I must make my will. Fred has his home for me to read. Do they have to have a red seal on to be legal? His hasn't any. How's your diet? I was going to give up cookies for lent but today noon I finished the cookies I had here since last Wed. I must have eaten 8. Poor me.

Your tent looks nice — I hope it's easy to put up — that's one of the nice parts about ours — you'll sleep crosswise — we sleep lengthwise. I wonder if you'll like being crosswise as well — the 3rd one might find it tough crawling over the other 2 if they have to get up in the middle of the nite — Fred says it will be ok, it's just different. And you may find it roomier then ours. The thing we like really well about ours is the putting up of the outside bars — so easy to hook up in a hurry. If yours are inside you might find it harder but it's all what you get use to. We like our windows but then again you don't need a lot cept if it's really hot and you're staying put in a spot for ages — windows would be nicer. We must write for dope now — I must do that tomorrow if I don't get going today.

Sally got a chain with a pearl from Don for her birthday and he sent her a card that said on it "with all my love, Don." The pearl was in a white jewellery box — with a sad looking white-haired cat on the cover. Must have gotten it in a jewellery store. Sally wore it this morning — she was so happy — she's more like herself these days — pills must be helping — she's eating and sleeping better. She takes liver pills and appetite pills and she's eating more but she still is skinny.

I'm anxious to have Bill come back, we miss him — food isn't eaten with him away.

Love, Ruby

Mar. 4/59

Dear Mum

Bill sent us a card — it looks exciting. I made a chocolate fudge cake for Sally's birthday and I'm baking bread today. Gee mum, is Fred ever nice to me — never goes out the door in the morning without kissing me and telling me to take care of myself. I guess I sure told him off. Sally is nice too. Helps me with dishes without me asking — though I seldom ever did that. She says good-bye now. Other mornings she'd go out the door without a word. No one has gotten cross or said a word or raised a voice since that talkout.

More snow tonite — Fred has so much ice in front of garage door that the bottom of the car almost hits it — he has to chop it away. Let's hope we won't be wet in the cellar when all this snow goes. Fred chopped out a wide trench to the drain in the floor so it should follow that and we shouldn't have any by rights.

Guess what I did? I went to a Jehova's witness meeting last nite — friend of Bill who was in public school with him asked me to go. His mother was there but she went with her boy friend and his mother. I went with Garry who had Mrs. Wilson drive us there and back. It was quite a meeting. I enjoyed it. They were so friendly and asked me to come again any time. They showed 1-1/2 films of a conference they have all over the world. Boy what a lot of followers they have. I didn't know they had so many in their gang. They don't believe in churches — Christ didn't have churches to preach in. Happiness is their main objective. There were 102 at the meeting — no one I knew — cept the chap at the corner who puts out the safety zone for the children and I made sure I didn't meet him or he'd be at my door to get me to be a Jehova. I enjoyed it but I wouldn't want to go again. It was interesting to see what they did and what it was about — Garry has always wanted me to go and his mother too and now I've been and that's that or they'll think I'm a prospect and I'll be pestered, eh? I'm not too anxious to get mixed up with them tho Garry and his mother are nice but that's all — just to speak to — not to get too friendly.

Love
Ruby

Mar. 6/59

Dear Jan

Do you care about people going to Florida? I don't. Look at Mabel
and Ches. — they went in Dec and Jan. and now they've all this snow to
fuss about still. Anyway we've been there and know what the place is like
and some day with out tents we can go again. It's more fun tenting then
moteling — you meet people you don't meet in motels — we met all
kinds — perfessors from N. Y. university and high school teachers — it's
fun — you'll love it — I'll eat my shirt if you don't. But Fred and I are
worried about all the miles — do you think we can hit Los Angeles? And
thro the desert — that worries me — Grahams said they drove through at
nite — in 112° heat — you can't go during the daytime — it's too
hot — you have to have lots of water with you and cars are all air
conditioned. Kath Hade had an aunt and uncle go down there and they
found the desert so hot they just couldn't take it — turned around and
came back.

There goes a car with 4 or 6 pairs of skis on top. Bill always says
they're going to Mt. Tremblant when he sees them pass like that. Fred
says we'll have to see how long it takes us to go to Yellostone — etc —
cause it's pretty far to Los Angeles then up the coast and across
Canada — you drive like mad on the road in the prairies — they're so
flat — you don't realize you're going fast and you get so sleepy.

My mat is getting scolapy — I've lost the nack of sewing. Oh I'm
having trouble and I don't want to rip it.

Save kid, gosh I haven't put a thing in the bank since just after
Xmas. I can't seem to save a penny — always something — yet I haven't
bought a thing or anything unnecessary.

What a party you were at — 400 people — wish I had that
dough — I'd spend it on seeing things, wouldn't you? Save, save
save — San Fransisco here we come.

They're putting gas lines up Young Street. What a gang of
machines, diggers, trucks etc etc. You really should see how fast they dig
ditches. They say it's going past our house — I hope on the other side of
the street. I'm too busy with rug to look up very often. I'll mail this this
aft — they have a post office in a store by the blinker.

Love
Ruby

Dear Mum

Bill is the Ontario Junior boys ski Champion. He's so pleased and thrilled. He beat Joe Dale who won the eastern Ontario Championship. Next winter they'll send him to Banff to try for the Canadian Olympic team. He's so happy. I guess the practice he had on his trip paid off — he had such a wonderful time, paid out of his own money. It cost him $100 but he bought stretchie pants for $25 — nice Austrian ones. I hope they're as good wearing as they are good looking. Bill told Fred he couldn't come down straight from the top of Stowe hills to the bottom — your legs get rubbery. He sorta got his fill. The hill at Stowe was really big and steep, you had to turn a lot, it was really tricky. One woman said "Damn that husband of mine making me come down this hill" Bill heard her — she was scared to death. There were piles of snow kicked up from turning that were dangerous. Bill fell several times.

I'm under the hair dryer now — 1st time I've really tried it since Fred gave it to me for Xmas. Sally uses it all the time and loves it — can't live without it now, can concentrate like mad under it, she says.

Mum, Fred is really wonderful — suggested we go out to see Bill ski — Sally helps me with the dishes without me asking for help — all's well — no fights or anything.

Can't hear the door being knocked or the phone ringing under the dryer wonder how long it takes to dry your head. Sally cut my bangs — hot's too hot — medium's ok. Bill has to write people in Montreal tonite to thank them. He's going to give Linda a present and a picture of himself — it was a picture the publicity people took of him to put in ski advertisements etc. Fred got two for Bill. You'll see it when we go home at Easter IF we go — depends on snow, etc. and water.

Bill's gone off to join a group at the church and Sally is studying. She's on a Hi Y discussion panel tomorrow with a mother, a teen-age boy and a father — the manager of the Barrie paper — discussing teenage problems — why go steady, etc. I'd like to hear it but at the same time Bill is playing in the school band at a Home and School nite at Barrie High with a discussion on what your child should take at University. Which one should I go to — I want to go to both. Which oh which????

My hair dried in 1/2 an hour.

Love Ruby

Dear Jan

Cheer up, nobody saves these days — they just do without and take important things first. Out west is more important then slip covers or a cement driveway — they both will wear out and a trip you'll remember for life — cheer up — everyone spends their income nowdays — there are very few who really save — only saving we did this month was not feeding Bill — we sure noticed a difference when he was away — not nearly as much milk or bread — fish lasted 2 meals instead of one. Food bills were cheaper — but we wouldn't want him away.

Gee kid, you can make yourself sick thinking of all the things you need and want — I did — and I gave it up — Gosh I can write a list of things we need and I'd like — cement driveway — new curtains, a new dress, set laundry tubs, new kitchen sink, new blankets, new spring coats for Sally and me — new hat for Fred. Hairdresser every two weeks, new kitchen storm door — ours cracked up in Hazel hurrycane — oh I could go on and on but I only think of our trip and buy only thread for my rug and no curtains, no cement driveway — for years I've wanted that — those awful stones walking into the place — but I'd rather go west wouldn't you then to not go? Gee we'll have so much fun — a sink is a sink and I've lived with a horrid one this long and the stones can keep on a few more years. They'll not be nice memories like a trip would be — who wants to look back when you're 80 and say what a nice sink and cement driveway we had — who cares — a trip seeing mountains and stuff would be nicer to think of — forget about all those things you need and plan our trip west. We must write for maps — now's the time. Everyone's tripping. The women around here plan a bus trip every year — last year Cape Cod, this year Florida or New York — but who wants to go with them without your family — sharing these things with ones you love is what makes the trip fun. Bill's really looking forward to the trip — seeing mountains. I wonder if we'll get to Los Angeles — it's really pretty far — but we'll see. Aren't you excited? Don't let this saving worry you — you'll get sick. Make Judy wear her old clothes. Sally wears that old blue skirt of Judy's and it's her favorite one right now. I'm not buying things — everything has to do. You have to clamp down on kids — they want everything.

Love Ruby

March 16/59

Dear Jan

I hope you're not cross at me for what I wrote yesterday about saving money. But I just don't want you to worry about not getting this and that — those things can wait — the Brukes have furniture like ours and they want to take it to their cottage and get new stuff but he couldn't even buy new ski pants cause he didn't have enough money — his are patched but he went on that trip to go skiing, that was far more important to him then new pants.

Just stop buying Judy and Tommy things — such as cookies — my kids won't eat sweets and I seldom have desert — an orange, apple, banana but no cakes — I made a cake for Sally's birthday and 1/3 is still sitting in the cake dish mother gave me for Xmas. Sally made a sauce to put on it on Friday to eat it up — I baked it Wed. — see — they don't want cake and cookies, a good dinner is what they like best. Try to get away from deserts — they cost lots and they're not good for you anyway. Just make you fat.

Don't worry — Fred doesn't make near as much as Harry and we're going west. I figure it will cost about $400 but it will be well spent. We hope to do it in less. We did our trip down east for about $200 for gas and food and toles for bridges stuff and all the things we bought, but I'll not buy stuff again — you don't need souvenirs. The trip is the main thing — to see things that you can remember the rest of your life.

I think Sally has really got the idea. She never asks for stuff any more. She said to me once she feels our money is like her money — we're one — can't spend stuff that's unnecessary — feels terrible if she thinks she's wasting. She's really good. Bill spends his own money and Sally does her's but she's more apt to use ours if she can. But not now since we're planning the trip. She understands.

Don't worry kid, we're in the boat with you. I often think a month away from here will seem ages — I wonder who'll look after the house when we're gone. Ches and Mabel go west in June, the Rogers go to the east coast when we're gone. We'll have to find somebody or we'll come back to a hay field in our front yard. Maybe we should get a sheep. Don't worry, we'll manage, someone will come. Maybe we'll rent it. More money for gas. San Franscisco here we come.

Love, Ruby

Addendum

by Edna Staebler

Sorry I stopped editing Ruby's letters so abruptly: everyone who has read them wants to know if the two families went with their tents to California and what happened after. Of course they went; they still talk about it (and they both have cement driveways now as well).

In 1963 Ruby's husband died suddenly of a heart attack. Two weeks later Sally graduated from the University of Toronto, and a year after that she married her steady, Don Reid, now a professor at York University. After their three children were born, Sally earned a Master's degree and taught math at Princeton, Rochester, Washington, York, Boston and Adelaide, wherever Don was invited to lecture.

Bill is now a family physician and chief of staff at a hospital in the Okanagan Valley of British Columbia. He has a wife, four young children, two cats, a dog, a house with a swimming pool, and a ski chalet on one of his beloved mountains.

Ruby still writes letters to Jan and me two or three times a week. She lives alone in her little white house, now surrounded by streets of other houses. She kept her job at the store for nine years after Fred died, then worked part-time at the local history museum and took night school courses in art.

Though fame and fortune have eluded her, her dreams of travel have come true. She has visited her pen pal in England, had a tour of Europe and another of the Holy Land, Greece, and Egypt (where she didn't run into Abraham). With Jan and me she went to New Zealand, Australia, and Hawaii, and last summer on a cruise to Alaska with her friend Mabel (age 90).

Edna Staebler is an award-winning journalist and has been a regular contributor to *Maclean's*, *Chatelaine*, and many other magazines. She is the author of *Cape Breton Harbour*, *Places I've Been and People I've Known*, and the *Schmecks* cookbook series.

Ruby keeps socializing with many friends, playing bridge, watching TV, and making catnip-filled knitted mice which have brought ecstasy to more than 30,000 cats all around the world.

A few weeks ago Ruby — now 84 — drove the 160 miles from her house to my cottage. We talked about her letters.

"Rube, when the book is published you'll be an author," I told her. "You'll be able to join the Writers' Union and the Canadian Authors' Association."

Her look was incredulous.

I said, "And you'll probably have to have your picture taken for the cover of the book."

"Oh gosh," Ruby looked nervous, then wistfully she said, "Do you think I'll get fan mail?"

Afterword

by Marlene Kadar

Haven't Any News: Ruby's Letters from the Fifties is a significant contribution to the reclamation of Canadian women's "ordinary voices." Housewives, too, have stories to tell, and although expert readers may not be used to these stories, they are the readers who can benefit from this reclamation. I think of my own reader position. Here I am reading Ruby's private mail. I read about the thoughts and feelings sisters and daughters share with each other and with their mother. This is complicated because none of the letter writers had the expectation at the time of writing that you and I would be privy to their secret messages, especially over a long period of time. We witness that the messages communicated through the past act like a glue, binding the writers to each other and to relationships established in their first family. For Ruby, moreover, the letters are also testimony to her role in the family and the household she is managing as she writes. Thus we can envision two large and engaging stories. In one Ruby tells about the life she lives in the present—in the 1950s in Ontario when 70 per cent of the households were managed by full-time housewives.[1] In the other she communicates through the act of writing itself, the way all narrators do; the letters tell an engaging story about the family into which Ruby was born, a story she tries to preserve in special relationships with other women. These two large stories intersect; the latter frames the former, as it does in any frame narrative. In other words, we are pulling story after story out of a housewife's rendering of her "ordinary" life, a life which is con-

---

Marlene Kadar teaches in the Humanities Division at York University. She is the editor of two important works on life writing, *Reading Life Writing* and *Essays on Life Writing: From Genre to Critical Practice*.

structed in personal and private letters. The correspondence is absorbing, as a novel is absorbing. But this is not the end of the story.

Ruby's letters tell about her everyday life and longings, through the central roles of homemaker, mother, wife, daughter, sister, paid store clerk, and, finally, writer. In these roles readers encounter an unusual and poignant narrator: the housewife we rarely meet in published works, speaking in her own voice, and not through the voice of a professional novelist. With some imagination the letters can be read as if they composed an epistolary narrative, one, perhaps, with some fashionable gaps and near-postmodern delays, and certainly without closure.[2]

Ruby's life stories are told in intimate letters to the women in her first family—letters which have been saved and edited by one of Ruby's correspondents, her sister, the well-known writer, Edna Staebler. The prose is casual, simple, and "ordinary," and as such does its part in what is now a feminist project to reclaim women's lives and writing during the period of the postwar "boom" era in Canada. As women's life writing, the letters document features of women's lives such as "drifting" ("life just happened to me") and "contingency" (women's lives depend on relationships) so aptly described in *Few Choices*, a study in which scholars Anne Duffy, Nancy Mandell, and Norene Pupo analyze women's lives in Canada on the basis of how they balance family and work. Ruby's letters, unassuming and authentic, representing the real stuff of women's lives, echo these themes. As women's life writing they also illustrate the literary patterns of overt and covert stories, of textual and subtextual meaning.

Overt Story: Women in the 1950s

There are at least five overt primary story-themes embedded in this collection of letters, themes which operate on the surface and which we can also call "everyday" evidence of the culture of everyday life for many women in Canada in the 1950s. The first has to do with Ruby's love of food and her anxiety about eating too much of it. As we learn from contemporary feminist analysis, the goodness of food transforms into a kind of negative longing: "I must not eat." As we know from Suzy Orbach (*Fat Is a Feminist*

Issue) or Eva Szekely (*Never Too Thin*), modern women think that they can never be too thin and, like Ruby, can punish themselves for eating too much. Ruby proclaims: "I can't get thin. I'm so fat, people tell me 'Oh you're fatter.' Darn. I can't eat NOTHING. I'm always hungry and I keep saying I won't eat but I eat twice as much" (p. 105). Sometimes Ruby's ambivalent joy in food is married to her interest in her daughter's social life, as when she prepared an opulent table for a party at which "those kids didn't eat a thing!" (p. 143).

The second theme has to do with the raising of Ruby's children, Sally and Billy, as they grow into their teen years. Ruby readily admits to Kay that the children do absorb her: "that's enough of Bill and his skiing and Sally and her party" (p. 144). Ruby seems at times to be more absorbed by Sally than Billy, however, and tends to criticize Sally more often. So there is a unique tension between the mother and daughter which does not exist between the mother and son. This tension is sharpened because the mother presents her daughter to the reader in her relations with boys — as above at the party — painting a unique portrait of the drama of sexual politics in the 1950s in which Sally is on stage, and the mother is waiting in the wings. The stories about Sally's sexual conquests are corroborated by fascinating recollections of the narrator's and her sisters' youth, and of running commentaries about mothers and children. The stories enmesh in the narrative, as in a letter to mum in which Ruby, speaking dispassionately about Sally's boyfriend, says: "Comes from a nice family but don't worry, Sally isn't marrying him — one doesn't stay with one beau forever — least I didn't" (p. 110). Ruby repeats that Sally will not marry yet.

The third theme has to do with women's work. Here Ruby's life in the letters can be viewed in its two major aspects: homemaking vs. clerking. A component of Ruby's homemaking is the creative life that revolves around handicrafts, especially rug-making. This women's work at home that is central to the life over which Ruby has power and makes choices is transformed into another kind of women's work, paid work in clerking, where she has less power. Ruby's acceptance of this paid work can be construed as a turning point in the epistolary narrative. In a series of run-on sentences Ruby agonizes over her new role as a paid worker at Musser's store: "I'm so scared. I'll have to make change and fit people and be on my feet all those hours — and what will Fred say when . . . I tell him?" (p. 58).

The fourth theme has to do with cats and other animals, such as dogs, birds, and squirrels. Ruby is especially taken with the fecundity of animals, and the sexual habits of female cats in particular. This interest can be read metaphorically. Ruby's interest in felines parodies her subtextual interest in sex and sexual politics in general, including her personal appearance.

The fifth theme has to do with personal appearance. Like every good woman in the 1950s, Ruby cares about her personal appearance, but not only her weight and body shape. She cares also about her wardrobe and the money she needs to spend in order to replace old coats or dresses which have become tight or out of fashion. As Ruby proclaims to Kay, "Haven't any news — saw a fashion show last nite — makes one feel sorta dowdy seeing such lovely clothes" (p. 31).

Covert Story: Feminist Subtexts

More interesting than the primary story-themes are the covert themes that bubble just under the surface of the linear time frame of the letter sequence. These themes function as overdetermined subtexts that indicate subaltern literary and political themes, or the bold *longings* of "a 1950s housewife" who hasn't "any news" (p. 31). These longings are wrapped around three interconnected subtexts which can be summarized as:

1. Ruby longs to have more money so she can buy more things, but also so she doesn't have to worry so much about the future for her children and for herself, i.e., "I wish we had money" (p. 87); she often wonders: how can I make more money?

2. Ruby longs to be a creative person, a person who makes a living creating story, especially by writing or painting. Occasionally she feels unsupported in this longing: i.e., "I wrote a story about our squirrels but I can't find the first part. Fred doesn't encourage me — I guess he doesn't think I'm any good, but at least I try and I keep sketching things too . . . to get the fear feeling out of your system" (p. 89). Although she does not give up on writing, Ruby does not give herself full permission to be the writer she imagines.

3. The (spiritual?) absence of the husband/lover/male peer bespeaks a longing for companionship (with the sisters? with the mum?) or "passed love" (p. 106). This particular longing is echoed in all of the stories which reveal the narrator's views about sex and love.

A Kind of Epistolary Narrative

As reclaimed life writing, the letters form an alternative to the so-called Literary letters that tell the same kind of story of love and longing, such as those we find in the tradition of the epistolary novel that stretches from *Pamela* by Samuel Richardson, to *Dear Diego* by Elena Poniatowska. These Literary letters are not only constructed, but the voices of the narrator and the letter writer are not one and the same. Sometimes they are not even the same gender. Richardson, for example, though not a woman, used a woman's voice to construct his view of proper virtue from which his own sexual longing can be deduced. Similarly, Poniatowska is not Angelina, the letter-writer, but she imitates Angelina's voice in order to construct the longing of the unrequited lover who becomes an artist in spite of herself. Whether Literary or otherwise, life writing allows a narrator to both construct a role and interrogate it, gracefully, in a way that may not be possible in real life.

In the end we have documents that reveal the aspirations of an (ordinary) woman writer, constructing herself much as other women writers do, but without any prior planning. There is a certain amount of genuine not-knowing-what-will-come-next between the lines. This natural suspense in this apparently epistolary narrative is constructed as a consequence of the passing of time and the naive development of a plot, the plot of everyday living. Through this plot, the reader is propelled in at least two ways. Primary themes carry the reader from letter to letter with some (temporal) unity; but the subtextual longings underwrite the entire correspondence and give it a writerly unity and depth. The letters are, as the narrator says, a kind of "dreaming" (p. 106).

Interruptions and Longing

It is interesting that the narrator's self-representation is occasionally interrupted by rages — as when Billy's tooth went through his tongue — and occasionally by meditative prose — as when the narrator constructs herself as artist, albeit the artist as a middle-aged housewife whose husband may not approve (p. 89). These illuminating sorties outside the normal range of emotion depicted in most of the letters emphasize that letters are not only the site of communication, but of self-presentation and affirmation. Thus, it is possible to read these letters as a kind of surreptitious affirmation of the dream of self as artist or writer. The beautiful irony is that the dream has come true; that the housewife *does* have news.

I see this real-life correspondence as a form of unpretentious interrogation of the norms and standards we apply to Great Literature, from which most women have been excluded. It answers the questions Joanna Russ posed ironically in 1983 in *How to Suppress Women's Writing*: what on earth can women write? why on earth don't they write Nobel prize-winning novels? where are all the Rubys and Ednas of the world? and, who exactly can be a writer? In order to welcome women into the academy, the academy needs to listen to women like Ruby. True, Ruby's writing does not vie with the canons of Great Literature but, in communicating with her loved ones, Ruby unwittingly writes her life into her personal letters and, almost accidentally, these letters make story. Ruby's lack of self-consciousness about writing becomes an advantage to the construction and deconstruction of identities, not a disadvantage. As Leonore Hoffmann and Margo Culley have illustrated in *Women's Personal Narratives*, the letter represents an important component part of women's vernacular literature.

The letter is, happily, a short and accessible genre; it does not require that the author have a host of degrees, a distinguished and unified "autobiographical" self (cf. Neuman, 214), or a pedigree. And finally, it can be squeezed into those few minutes between baking the bread, minding the children, and getting to work on time.

Notes

1 See Bonnie Fox, "Women's Double Work Day: Twentieth-Century Changes in the Reproduction of Daily Life," in *Hidden in the Household*, 216.
2 For the features of postmodern fiction, see Linda Hutcheon, *A Poetics of Postmodernism*.

Works Cited

Culley, Margo. "Women's Verncaular Literature: Teaching the Mother Tongue." *Women's Personal Narratives*. Ed. Leonore Hoffman and Margaret Culley. New York: Modern Language Association of America, 1985. 9-17.

Duffy, Ann, Nancy Mandell, and Norene Pupo. *Few Choices: Women, Work and Family*. Network Basics Series. Toronto: Garamond, 1989.

Fox, Bonnie, ed. *Hidden in the Household: Women's Domestic Labour under Capitalism*. Toronto: Women's Press, 1980.

Hoffmann, Leonore, and Margaret Culley, eds. *Women's Personal Narratives: Essays in Criticism and Pedagogy*. New York: Modern Language Association of America, 1985.

Hutcheon, Linda. *A Poetics of Postmodernism: History, Theory, Fiction*. New York and London: Routledge, 1988.

Neuman, Shirley. "Autobiography: From Different Poetics to a Poetics of Differences." *Essays in Life Writing: From Genre to Critical Practice*. Ed. Marlene Kadar. Toronto: University of Toronto Press, 1992. 213-30.

Orbach, Susie. *Fat Is a Feminist Issue*. New York: Berkley Books, 1985.

Poniatowska, Elena. *Dear Diego*. Trans. Katherine Silver, 1978. New York: Pantheon, 1986.

Richardson, Samuel. *Pamela; or Virtue Rewarded*. 1740. Harmondsworth: Penguin, 1980.

Russ, Joanna. *How to Suppress Women's Writing*. Austin: University of Texas Press, 1983.

Szekely, Eva. *Never Too Thin*. Toronto: Women's Press, 1988.